powered by
FEEL

**How Individuals, Teams
and Companies Excel**

powered by

FEEL

How Individuals, Teams and Companies Excel

James G S Clawson
University of Virginia, USA

Doug Newburg
University of Florida Medical School, USA

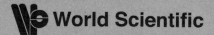

World Scientific

NEW JERSEY · LONDON · SINGAPORE · BEIJING · SHANGHAI · HONG KONG · TAIPEI · CHENNAI

Published by

World Scientific Publishing Co. Pte. Ltd.

5 Toh Tuck Link, Singapore 596224

USA office: 27 Warren Street, Suite 401-402, Hackensack, NJ 07601

UK office: 57 Shelton Street, Covent Garden, London WC2H 9HE

Library of Congress Cataloging-in-Publication Data
Clawson, James G.
  Powered by feel : how individuals, teams, and companies excel / by James G.S. Clawson &
Douglas S. Newburg.
    p. cm.
  Includes bibliographical references.
  ISBN-13: 978-981-281-892-8 (pbk)
  ISBN-10: 981-281-892-8 (pbk)
  1. Performance--Psychological aspects.   I. Newburg, Douglas S.   II. Title.
  BF481.C485 2007
  650.1--dc22

                                            2008049859

British Library Cataloguing-in-Publication Data
A catalogue record for this book is available from the British Library.

ISBN-13 978-981-281-892-8 (pbk)
ISBN-10 981-281-892-8 (pbk)

In-house Editor: Juliet Lee Ley Chin

Printed in Singapore by World Scientific Printers

DEDICATION

We dedicate this book to those who were subjects in Doug's research and ethnographic interviews over the last 15 years. This includes more than 550 people who come from at least five major different disciplines including athletics, medicine, music, business, and the military. They include individualists and strong team players, people who wear warm-ups and three-piece suits, people who make a lot of money and people who don't care much about money, people who are brown, black, and white, people who work on water and on land, and who come from every corner of the earth. What they have in common is that they have excelled in their professions, they have demonstrated their ability to perform at the world-class level. We are grateful for their willingness to share their experience and stories with us so that we all might learn.

JAMES PREFACE

I spent most of my life suppressing my feelings and ignoring them in order to do what was necessary to accomplish things I thought I was supposed to do. This so-called achievement orientation in some respects served me well. I was able to graduate with great distinction from Stanford University, earn a doctorate at the Harvard business school, and eventually become a chaired full professor at the University of Virginia. I felt active, intellectually, physically, socially, spiritually, and societally. I became a leader in my church, and I was active in a consulting practice that took me around the world. Somewhere along the way, though, I began to feel empty inside. This was hugely ironic for me since I had spent my life doing things that I was told and which I believed were of great value and of lasting impact.

One day I woke up feeling deep despair because I felt further behind than I had the day before: further behind with my health, with my family, with my work, with my charity work, basically on every aspect of life. I looked at the next day and the next week and the next month and the next year, and I couldn't see how anything would change. It wasn't so much that I was blindsided by this, since I have been a student of human development and behavior since my studies at Harvard. I was aware of the transitions that people typically go through in life and of the stages of professional careers. But somehow things weren't turning out the way everyone said they would. My assumed strategy of "do what you're told and do it really well" was working on the outside but not on the inside.

One of my pleasures in life had been playing basketball. I began playing in the third or fourth grade in Boise, Idaho. I made the high school basketball team but didn't start. I played on all-church basketball teams, but never won. In a pickup game in Cambridge, MA in the Cage once, the former starting point guard for the Stanford University varsity team, told me that I played extremely good defense. It was the kind of thing I would never forget, but which would never appear on my resume. So, I was good enough to enjoy the sport, but never good enough to make it a profession.

When I moved to the University of Virginia, one of the first things I did was find the noontime pickup game. Every university has one. I played in that game until I was physically unable to do so. One day, I had a very challenging matchup. I took a shot and he blocked it. I made a pass and he stole it. I tried to block him and he swished it over me from 40 feet. (Yes, *40* feet.) My frustration on the court led to a series of conversations off the court which have blossomed into an extremely rewarding professional and personal relationship. The guy I was checking was Doug Newburg, former varsity basketball player for the University of Virginia who played with Ralph Sampson during the glory days of Virginia basketball. Our conversations quickly went from basketball to a variety of other topics. One day he invited me to come listen to him give a lecture in the psychology department, and my life was changed.

Doug had spent 15 years interviewing world-class performers in multiple industries. The insights he has drawn from that research have been for me extraordinary. We had been talking for a couple of years about writing a book together. When we decided to begin, it was clear to him and then to me, that outlining the book, and then each chapter and then slogging through the writing was not going to be enjoyable or rewarding for either of us. So, he made what I thought was a brilliant suggestion. He said why don't we play pickup basketball as we write? Like we do on the court and like we do when we present.

We had taught together before, and the times when it went best were the times when we were the most organic and unstructured. Like playing catch. So we decided to try this as we wrote the book. There may be other volumes written in this way, but I have never seen them. I can say this, it was extremely inspiring and rewarding to write in this way. I found myself eagerly awaiting Doug's response to each of my chapters. When his would arrive by e-mail, typically I would read it and began writing a response immediately. This has been at the same time the easiest and most emotionally demanding volume I have ever written.

We hope that this conversation in print will help you understand more deeply and profoundly than you have about the relationship between how you feel and how you perform. We've become convinced that it is one of the most overlooked, underrated, underestimated relationships in virtually all aspects of life: especially in organizational life. At the end of the book, we invite your comments, suggestions and communications. We look forward to hearing from you and including you in our conversations.

Acknowledgments

Every published work is the result of the hard work of many people. Of course, my primary acknowledgment goes to Doug for the time he's taken in the course of his life to share with me his insights and thinking. We are also grateful to Max Phua of World Scientific Publishing for his interest in and trust in our content and our unusual process. Juliet Lee has been wonderful in editing and refining the appearance of the volume. Marcia Conner, whom we asked to review an early manuscript, went above and beyond to offer suggestions in a very detailed way. We also thank

Dr. Craig Smith, Dr. Mehmet Oz, Professor Randolph New, Art Glenn, W. Tanner Stewart, Bob Johnson, and Susan Clawson for their willingness to review the manuscript and offer suggestions.

I'm also grateful to the Darden Graduate School of Business, the Research Committee, and the Darden Foundation, for their support during my professional activities as we wrote this volume. Barbara Richards and Kathy Shelton at the Darden Graduate School of Business were very helpful in printing and editing various versions of the manuscript.

We also acknowledge those world-class performers who took time out from their busy lives to interview with Doug and share their insights with the rest of the world. I'm also grateful to my wife Susan, who puts up with a lot of strange behavior.

James G. S. Clawson
Charlottesville, Virginia
June 22, 2008

DOUG PREFACE

When Jim and I agreed to write this book together, I believed there were a couple of reasons that this made good sense. First, Jim has listened to or presented with me dozens of times. After some initial years of those joint presentations not going exactly as we hoped, we started doing more of a talk-show interview format. Jim would open with a case that would lead to my research. All of a sudden it was really fun to present as we went back and forth as Jim said "playing pickup."

Jim has presented my research to more organizations and more groups than I have. My hope in creating this book with him is to capture what he learned in sharing my work in his own way. We come at this work from very different backgrounds and places.

While he has presented my work around the world, I have worked one-on-one with people and companies in intensive, sometimes long-term, consulting engagements helping these individuals and organizations become world-class. My hope for this book was to combine my research with the teaching and consulting lessons from both Jim and I. I wanted to share with you what I believe makes the difference between world-class and mediocre and what you can do about it.

That was my idea for this book — that by combining our experiences, we could make this information accessible and useful to you.

As you read, I hope you will keep that thought in mind. In the final chapter, I share what I learned writing the book, and it might be the most important lesson of all.

My objective is to make what I learned accessible to you, to invite you to give it consideration, and do what *you* feel. The only way I know to do that, what I have done in my writing, is to tell you almost exactly what I say to someone with whom I am working one-on-one.

What I hope you will *feel* reading the book is my love for what I do. I love the puzzle, the inquiry, the listening, the late-night conversations with world class performers or those still striving. I love watching people feel how they want to feel, especially when I helped them find it. Nothing is more important to me, nothing calls to me louder. In the book *Seeing is Forgetting the Name of the Thing You See*, author Lawrence Weschler describes Robert Irwin as "an artist who one day got hooked on his own curiosity and decided to live it."

My wish for you is that you feel the call that is yours and then answer it. I hope this book helps you do so more easily.

Doug S. Newburg
Gainesville, Florida
July 10, 2008

CONTENTS

MANAGING FEEL IN ORGANIZATIONS

PERSONAL APPLICATIONS

FUNDAMENTAL CONCEPTS

LEONARDO daVINCI

ALL OUR KNOWLEDGE PROCEEDS FROM WHAT WE FEEL.

PICK UP

*T*ony Athos had been on the cover of *Time* magazine as one of the country's best teachers. When I arrived at the Harvard Business School as a doctoral student, he was a senior faculty member. For some reason, he looked kindly on me and took me under his wing. Later as a member of the faculty, teaching a course he designed, I asked him to come watch me teach which he agreed to do. I was up half the night preparing my teaching plan, board plan, contingency plans, key questions, etc. I really wanted to impress him. He sat in the back, and I taught my class. Afterward, I ran down to his office, salivating like Odie the dog, looking for feedback. I sat down … and he said, "Jim, you're boring." THUNK! An arrow to the heart. My mouth went dry, my palms were sweaty, and I whispered, "Okay, tell me about boring."

"I notice you play basketball with the doctoral students at noon."

"Yes, I love basketball."

"Well, it's obvious. When you come back, your face is lit up, you're grinning from ear to ear, and you're floating down the hall three inches off the floor. You've got to figure out how to play basketball in the classroom."

I remember thinking at that moment, "That's not right. This is work and basketball is play." I went away depressed and frustrated. And I kept

musing on his comment. I thought about it more and more. Well, there *is* a tipoff, you have to start somehow. And you pass the "ball" to a student with a question. If students were prepared, they'd catch it. If not, they'd drop it or it would bounce off their foreheads, BRONG, out of bounds. So, you'd pass to someone else. They might catch it, dribble around for a minute, maybe dribbling too much, and finally pass it to someone else. Every now and then, someone would make an insightful comment, really cutting to the heart of the case or issue, like a reverse slam dunk, people would cheer, and we'd move off "down the court" in another direction. The "ball" was the opportunity to speak, like Native American speaking sticks. When the section worked together, the discussion was a beautiful thing to watch, just like a well orchestrated team, moving the ball quickly and efficiently. Good discussion points, like basketball points, came fast and furious. You *could* play basketball in the classroom.

I began working on that principle in my teaching. I talked less. I coached more. I nodded, I glanced, I raised my eyebrows, and the students began to pick up on these gentle signals and exercise their own heads and energies. The classroom began to come alive for me. It was more and more fun to watch them play rather than trying to control their every movement. When I left HBS, my student ratings had climbed to second in the school. To this day, I attribute much of whatever I might enjoy about teaching to two main mentors, first, Tony and then, Sherwood (who taught the doctoral seminar on pedagogy at Harvard Business School and became a lifelong friend and colleague). While I didn't know it at the time, Tony had given me a glimpse of a principle I wouldn't really discover until I was 48, some 16 years later.

When I came to the University of Virginia, one of my first goals was to find the local basketball game. They played at Memorial Gym then, but over the years it migrated to the latest, newest of the university's recreation facilities. I met people in that daily 11 am–1 pm game who have become lifelong friends. Dick, Craig, Gary, Elliott, and a host of others. At the time, Ralph Sampson and the Cavaliers were on a rampage, winning, as it turned out, more games in their four years than any other team in NCAA history.

Fifteen years later, I was still playing in the noon-time game. Get there early or you miss the first one and have to wait. Don't miss your foul shots or you have to sit. Try to hook up with the better players so you don't have to sit. Ten pushups before every game to warm up the triceps. Games to 11 by ones, win by two. The coaches were always strong, several from the football team, the basketball team and the soccer team. Some were very intense, win at any cost kind of guys. Tom O'Brien was always the perfect gentleman. He played hard and was also a gentleman. I had to guard Bruce Arena often as we had similar builds and speed or lack thereof. One day, there was a guy I'd never seen before. I played "2" usually, had a good jumper. I went up against this new guy and bang! "Spaulding" was tattooed on my forehead. I faked and passed — he stole the ball in mid air. I picked him up at the half court line, he took two steps over, picked up his dribble, looked both ways, elevated and "swish," nothing but net. We lost 11-1. Jeez. Who was that guy?

"Oh," Dick said. "That's Doug Newburg. He played with Sampson. Didn't play much. Went away and came back."

I played on the same court with Doug quite a bit that summer. Then one day, he sidled up and said, "I do more than play basketball. Would you mind if I came to talk with you in your office?" We talked at the Darden School for an hour and Doug told me about his emerging research on world-class performance. He'd been interviewing Olympic gold medalists, world record holders, touring musicians, business people, and naval aviators. He'd observed a common pattern in how they approached their lives and told me about what he'd seen. He asked me if I wanted to come to a lecture he was giving in the psych department that night.

I went and sat on the back row. There were maybe 500 students in the lecture hall. Doug began his talk. The word "resonance" came up a lot. About halfway through, he asked a question at which I was dumbstruck. NO ONE had ever asked me that question before. Not my mom, not my dad, none of my teachers, none of my supervisors, none of my clients, no one … ever. I couldn't answer it.

How do you want to feel?

I went home that night and couldn't sleep. All my life I'd been taught that what counted was what you *did*. Did you do your homework? Did you clean your plate? Did you mow the lawn? Did you clean your room? What did you get on your report card? Did you go to work? Did you finish your term paper? Did you read the book? Did you get a job? Did you finish your application? Did you get in? Did you get your degree? Did you publish anything this year? Did you teach your courses?

I graduated with Great Distinction from Stanford University. That's Summa Cum Laude in other schools. I'd received my MBA from Brigham Young University and had gone to work in San Francisco at Wells Fargo.

I rode the commuter train up and down the peninsula, past all the houses made out of ticky tacky. I remember crawling out of my water bed on the floor on my hands and knees to the shower reaching up to turn on the shower to wake up at 5 am in order to make the 6:14 am express. I wore suits; I analyzed credits. And I was dying. Every day I felt like they hooked a hose to my abdomen when I went in and sucked out a day's portion of my life's juices.

So, I went back to school. My first week in Cambridge, I slowed down for a yellow light in Harvard Square and some guy in a pickup rammed me from behind, pushed me through the intersection, cursed at me, and flipped me off. I realized I wasn't in Idaho any more. I got my doctorate and was privileged to be invited to join the faculty.

One day at a conference in Los Angeles I got in a little debate with a presenter. Unbeknownst to me the guy sitting next to me was from the Darden Graduate School of Business at the University of Virginia. The next month I got an invitation to visit; I didn't know where Charlottesville was. Tony had spoken highly of the school; I remembered that. During the interviews, they asked me about my family and recreational activities. That was a surprise.

At HBS the message was, "What have you done today?" Not yesterday, but *today*. It was a heady environment. Former Secretaries of Labor and Commerce walking around. World-class scholars and teachers. Enormous history. Wonderful colleagues, junior and senior. People who had written the books I was studying. At UVA, they used the case method, so I knew the classroom well. But they asked about my family. When I got back to Boston, one of my colleagues learned that after nine years he had not been granted tenure. That wasn't unusual. 90 percent of faculty who come, I was told, don't make it. This fellow went home, though, and shot himself. I began to wonder if I was at Harvard to be at Harvard or if I was there to be me. I surveyed my senior colleagues and concluded I'd likely make the associate hurdle but not the full one. So I left my appointment. One of my mentors told me no one had ever done that before, left before being asked to leave. I don't know.

But Charlottesville felt right, so I stayed. 16 years later, in the gym, I got Spaulding tattooed on my forehead. And the guy asked me a question I couldn't answer.

It took me eighteen months and some forty drafts to answer that question, *how do you* ***want*** *to feel?* It was one of those pivotal events in life that changes one's course. It changed my life. I may be a slow learner. And I'm aware of this: no one had asked that question before I met Doug.

GERRY LOPEZ

All it takes is one wave, not even that. One turn. Just a moment that keeps pulling you back to have another moment. And it never ends.

FEEL

*H*ow do you want to feel?

It seems like such a simple question. It seemed too simple to me as I interviewed hundreds of world class performers about their lives and careers expecting to hear about hard work and perseverance and goal setting. Those words were rarely spoken.

And yet they used that word over and over again. Feel.

I became interested in feel when I was working on my dissertation for my PhD in Sports Psychology. I was lucky enough to work with several world class performers — a swimmer, a drummer, a heart surgeon, a veterinarian, a woman college basketball player, Jim. They became friends of mine, good friends.

These connections were the key I never found in school, in the people who I was supposed to learn from, to listen to. These people were well educated with long lists of achievements, although in their own way, in their own time, they started asking me about themselves. They were curious about my work, about how athletes thought and trained, how they prepared. The conversation began.

We were all trained to think, to analyze, to dig deeper, to learn techniques in our own fields. Yet the conversation kept coming back to the experiences we had as children and as teenagers — that play required the same kind of discipline that our careers required. When we played with that discipline, we came alive, we felt *free*.

My dissertation focused on this feeling. When I thought and analyzed and had to come up with a thesis topic, I chose to focus on freedom. There was something about *freedom* that made world class performers better than other people. They had the freedom to act, think, train, learn in ways other people did not.

I was pretty full of myself. I was studying freedom, something important, philosophically challenging, testing myself. I set off to free the world. I asked everyone I knew, anyone who would listen, who would talk to me. "What is freedom?" and, "How do you define freedom?"

A month into the process, I already wanted to quit because almost without exception, people answered by describing a lack of boundaries or a lack of oppression rather than the qualities for freedom itself. I was missing something. I blamed the people I was asking for not being curious enough, for not thinking about freedom. It was boring and I was boring myself.

Then one day, an ultimate Frisbee player changed my perspective. He told he had no idea how to describe freedom. Then he went on to say, "I feel the most free when I am flying through the air diving after the Frisbee in the end zone."

That is how I discovered *feel*.

He was not thinking about flying through the air. He felt it. Right there in front of me. I saw it. *I felt it*. I felt it enough to want to go play Frisbee, to see what it was like. And now I understood what all those others had been trying to tell me, what I was to hear over and over again in my work. I heard what turned my work into play.

In interviewing hundreds of world class performers from a wide range of fields, I continued to hear the same thing over and over again. I felt the same thing over and over again.

When I asked people to explain how they came to be world-class, "How did you get where you are?" every one of them struggled with an intellectual explanation… but for a few moments in every conversation, they came alive. They lit up, sat forward, and *felt* what they did. They transcended their resumes, ignored their achievements. They told me their *stories*, stories defined not by what they did, but how it felt.

Let me now ask you the question: How do you want to feel?

Did you stop and ask "What is feel?" Probably not. Most people don't. In fact, it may seem like a silly question. They dismiss it as trivial, even irresponsible.

Almost no one ever asks me what I mean by *feel*.

"Does how you feel affect how you perform?"

Jim and I have asked hundreds of audiences and thousands of people this question. They nod and answer without hesitation a resoundingly "Yes!"

We then ask another question.

"When was the last time someone asked you at work (or anywhere else for that matter) how they could help you feel the way you want to or need to?"

Audiences break into laughter. When we ask why they are laughing, they say "No one."

Yet, they have all just agreed that how they feel affects how they perform. This means no one responsible for performances has offered to help them perform better or has even asked them if they could help them put feel to work.

I sat one day in a small meeting with the Vice President of a large organization. Ironically, she was the Vice President for Leadership Development. We went through this Q and A about feel. Did it affect performance? Yes. What did she do then for her employees, for the leaders she was in charge of developing as far as this feel that affected their performance?

She said "Nothing. It is not my responsibility."

Huh?

"You just said that how we feel affects how we perform?" I replied.

"Yes, but it's not my responsibility to my employees to worry about how they feel."

If you agree that how we feel affects how we perform, I would argue that to ignore *feel* is irresponsible. This is the dilemma Jim faced when he heard me ask the question. This is the opposite of what we are told growing up.

Yet, this is exactly what I heard in my interviews from some of the most successful people in the world.

The world-class performers I interviewed, the friends who started me down this path, even those I work with who seem to have lost their way all said the same thing I experienced talking to the Frisbee guy.

At some point in their lives, they *felt something* when they did whatever it is they chose as a career. They wanted to do it again and again and again. The more they did it, the better they got at it because they did it longer than people who worked at it. The better they got, the more they felt how they wanted to feel.

How do you want to feel?

BENJAMIN DISRAELI

NEVER APOLOGIZE FOR SHOWING FEELING.
WHEN YOU DO SO, YOU APOLOGIZE FOR
TRUTH.

Professionalism

PROFESSIONALISM

*C*learly they weren't getting it. As I looked around the room, most eyes were glazing over or exuding anger. Much like Doug's client in the previous chapter, but in aggregate. It was perplexing to me. The first time I heard Doug's explanation and discussion of feel, it hit a deep chord with me ... it resonated. But clearly that wasn't happening here. We were consulting with a client of mine and the session on resonance was not going well. They couldn't see the relevance of "feel" or "resonance" and the more we talked, the more irritated they got. The session ended unsatisfactorily. Many were confused, some were angry, a few genuinely inspired.

I wondered a lot about that session. It occurred to me that the participants in the session were having the same kind of reaction I'd had when Tony Athos told me I needed to learn how to play basketball in the classroom. At first I thought his advice was misguided, and the reason was because I believed that "work was work and play was play." In my mind they not only didn't mix, they were just different and separate parts of life.

Later, I learned about semi-conscious assumptions about the way the world is or should be. These assumptions shape the way we view the world and what we judge to be good or bad, functional or dysfunctional, acceptable or not. Ed Schein at MIT was instrumental in my seeing this.[1] His research that addresses one might apply cultural anthropology to an

---

[1] Schein, Edgar, *Organizational Culture and Leadership*, Jossey-Bass, San Francisco, 1985.

understanding of human behavior helped enormously. So did Albert Ellis' work on the relationship between rationality and emotion.[2]

I used these insights as I wondered why our client group had responded so negatively. I began to wonder what their underlying assumptions must have been to have the reactions they were having. After all, it's not new. The Stoics knew in 50 AD, for example that it's not the situation that affects a man's view, it's the view the man takes of the situation.

Then one day it occurred to me:

PWD WTHTD ROHTF

"Professionals will do what they have to do regardless of how they feel." It's a common assumption. In fact, it now seems central to me in most managerial assumptive schemes. Further, a variation on it dominates the thinking of most parents: "mature adults will do what they have to do regardless of how they feel." It's the definition of adulthood. It's what it means to be mature. It's the goal that most parents lay before their children as they watch them fuss about doing their homework, their chores, or applying to college. It is, it seems to me, the dominant assumption that most managers take as they offer jobs to people that they, without pay, otherwise might not be at all interested in doing.

What do you think? Have you heard that assumption taught to you before? Do you believe it? Are you thinking, "Of course?"

> Beware the assumption: "Professionals will do what they have to do regardless of how they feel."

This assumption, PWD WTHTD ROHTF, is a formula for mediocrity. First, this assumption moves people from choice to obligation and that's

---

[2] Ellis, Albert and Harper, Robert, *A Guide to Rational Living*, Wilshire Book Company, North Hollywood, CA, 1975.

a factor that reduces energy. Second, it encourages people to suppress or negate their feelings squelching the very thing that is a source of energy and passion.

When you take away choice and emotion, you end up with people who are complying or going through the motions. That's a process that leads to mediocrity.

If managers believe that professionals will do what they have to do regardless of how they feel, it's no wonder that the next step is trying to figure out how to "motivate" them.

There's a huge irony here: we manage people to work out of obligation and without emotion and then wonder why they aren't more motivated. Pressed by obligation and encouraged to suppress their feelings, the ideal mature, adult employee would be obedient, conforming, and predictably neutral, taking on any assignment given them, neither hot nor cold, lukewarm but productive.

This phenomenon is all the more remarkable when one watches kids before they enter school. I've asked adult managers all over the world what they did to entertain themselves before entering school and it's a common set of answers. They'd spend hours well past sundown playing with a cardboard box, a mud puddle, a wooden spoon, ant hills, a ball, and dirt. Mom might call out, "Time for dinner!" and the response was, "Just a few minutes more, Mom. I've got things to *do* out here!"

Somewhere along the way, all that innate energy and enthusiasm got squelched or sidetracked or stuffed.

J A M E S   T A Y L O R

THE SECRET OF LIFE IS ENJOYING THE PASSAGE OF TIME.

SUCCESS

*I*f you ask children of a certain age what they are doing, they simply respond "Playing" in a way that suggests it is a stupid question.

Soon they start playing a game and then a sport. They specialize, the day comes when they perform. Eventually they invite and receive judgment. They care more about winning and losing and what others think of them … and play becomes work so they stop *playing*. Most kids who do not measure up quit and find something else to do. Or worse, they avoid doing anything they might not be good at, avoid judgment, cower from feeling not good enough.

Something happens to the meaning of the word *game*. The games of our childhood allow us to learn, to grow, to develop. We come to know ourselves before we even know there is a self.

What's the adult version of the game? It's pleasing, measuring up, chasing the moving target provided by the approval of others. When we say we have to "play the game" we are not talking about an honorable pursuit. That game is defined by its lack of integrity, reliant on deceit. Consider this from the movie *Instinct*, based on the book *Ishmael*.

> *You asked me a question once. "What has you all tied up in knots when you wake up sweating in the middle of the night?" It's the game. l was so good at it. l made sure all the right people liked me. At night, I'd do the checklist in my mind. Am l cool with*

Ben Hillard? Am l cool with Dr. Josephson? Am l cool with all the people who can help me? Am l cool with all the people who can hurt me? Nobody thought l was weak or a loser. There was nobody l was offending, nobody l loved. That game, Ethan.

Childhood wonder, the awe of the world, and excitement from figuring things out gives way to the game we play as adults. The power to grow turns into the power to control.

I have talked with thousands of people about their lives and their careers, about the decisions they make. They each have their reasons for exchanging play for work. When I am asked to share my experience and help people *feel* better, I can predict that some time after we start talking they will utter the sentence, "I did everything I was supposed to do, but my life doesn't feel the way I thought it would."

My follow up: "How did you think life would feel?"

Free. They thought it would feel more *free*. And these people come from a wide swath of professions, success levels, backgrounds.

Most of us start down the path to success then become professionals to live the way we want. The social contract, our price to pay, is time and money spent training, obeying authority, being where someone else needs us to be. We give up certain rights in order to live more free, to live how we choose.

But something else happens along the way for many of us.

When I speak to executives in workshops, one of my visuals always silences the group. It's a ladder of success (Figure 4.1).

It implies that we get good grades so we can get into a good school, so we can get a good job so we can borrow the money to buy a car so we can get married so we can borrow the money to buy a house so we can have kids.

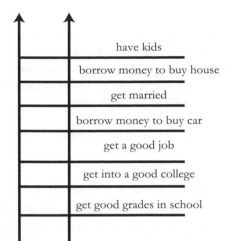

Figure 4.1. Success ladder (from the bottom up)

They sit silent, stunned. I explain people seek me out to work with because they have done all these things, achieved all these goals, and they have no idea what's next.

They have climbed this ladder, followed a prescribed path, started out with the best intentions. Somewhere along the path, though, too many people lose their way and because they didn't create the path themselves, and then they just do what's next.

Then I point out to the executives that not only do we pursue an acceptable ladder of goals, we lock into very narrow paths of responsibility, accepted by others whose approval we seek.

Consider this passage from *Boy's Life* by Robert MacCammon I came across in the Journal of the American Medical Association. A heart surgeon I worked for said this is the fear we see in many young men and young women who come into medical school. They are afraid we're going to take away their magic. Our job is to help them hold on.

"We all start out knowing magic. We are born with whirlwinds, forest fires, and comets inside of us. We are all born able to sing to birds and read the educated right out of our souls. We get it churched out, spanked out washed out, and combed out. We get put on the straight and narrow and told to be responsible. Told to act our age. Told to grow up for God's sake."

What defines success comes from outside of us and *how* we pursue success is prescribed to us.

When we have done everything we're supposed to do and we feel empty, a sense of betrayal sets in. We become lost and confused with nowhere to go, no way out. Like being seasick on a ship far from port.

Those still working on the ladder feel less than they thought they would become if they did what they were supposed to do. They kept their end of the bargain and it feels like a broken promise.

One founder of Netsys (which he sold for $95 million), now one of the top professional poker players in the world, said, *"I was living the American Dream ... and not my own."*

World-class performers told me they set their goals based on how they felt. They took risks of failure, of going against the wishes of others because how they felt when they were doing what they did was too compelling.

This takes us back to the question: "How do you want to feel?"

A Grammy award-winning musician told me loved how he felt making music so he decided to be a musician, a professional musician so he could afford to play music, to do what he loved.

An executive I interviewed had been in the Air Force with Chuck Yeager and Neil Armstrong, and he felt how much they loved and respected their work. He wanted to feel that way too, but he knew it would not happen in the Air Force. He went to business school, then on to New York and he came to love finance, specifically helping people put together companies and to lead young people to where they wanted to go in life. He retired several years ago as the International Chairman of Goldman Sachs.

Another executive told me:

> *"It is not like I said growing up that I want to be CEO of a big company. The model for me developed incrementally. At one point, I said I'd like to build this company to a billion dollars. That would be neat. The word vision may be better in this case. You can see it vs. just throwing something out there. The difference being that the vision takes hold of your attention, not just takes up your time. For me, the vision is that you want to be able to use your talents… The people who are not happy are the people who are not using all their talents."*

World-class performers did not choose goals that were a means to an end. They chose goals based on how *they* alone wanted to feel everyday. They did things they did not want to do in order to do more things they wanted to do.

Another Grammy-award winning musician said it this way when someone asked him in one of my classes how he kept from burning out:

> *"I don't confuse what I get paid to do. I get paid to travel, to be away from my family, to get dehydrated, to have the bus get lost on the way to a gig only to show up and my drums still need to be set up. Playing the drums? I play the drums for free."*

As a three time Olympic Gold Medalist told me:

> *"My goal is to win the Gold Medal in the Olympics. But the only reason that's my goal is because my dream is to play every day against the best competition and to play to win. When I'm playing to win, that's when I feel resonance. And if I win, that's great. I want to win; and having the Gold Medal as a goal forces me to play to win, but what I love to do, what my dream is, what this is for me is playing to win."*

Author Jacob Needleman said it this way, echoing what I heard in my interviews:

> *"To be totally engaged with all my functions, all my faculties, all my capacities in life. To me, that would be success."*

What is success for you? Does your definition include how it feels?

VIJAY SINGH

I'VE DONE WHAT I NEED TO DO, AND I HAVE
TO WORRY ABOUT WHAT I FEEL, AND NOT
ABOUT WHAT OTHER PEOPLE FEEL, AND I
FEEL GREAT ABOUT MY GAME, MYSELF, AND
WHAT I HAVE DONE.

Inside-Out

INSIDE-OUT

"How much of your life do you live inside-out versus outside-in?" That is, are you letting society define for you what success means or are you defining it yourself? Consider Figure 5.1. When we live outside-in, we are allowing the outside world to influence us. When we conform to the culture surrounding us, when we imitate those around us, when we censor what we otherwise would do or say because of our concerns about what others would say, we are living outside-in. When we say what we think, when we are honest with others, when we are transparent, when we do as we believe, we are living inside-out.

Most of us live far more outside-in than we realize. This is not necessarily bad since we need to conform to some degree in order to have society, civilization, language, organizations, and any kind of team work. The question is "To what degree?" Consider the scale on the left hand side of Figure 5.1. People who live their lives utterly outside-in or zero inside-out would be at the bottom. These we might call mindless, spineless, wishy-washy, without opinions, without personality. At the other extreme, those who might live all inside-out and have no room for the views of others we might call egotistic, self-centered, narcissistic, arrogant, SOBs. Few individuals live at either extreme.

There are at least two fundamental questions here. The first would be "Where do you fall, typically, on this scale?" That is, on average, where

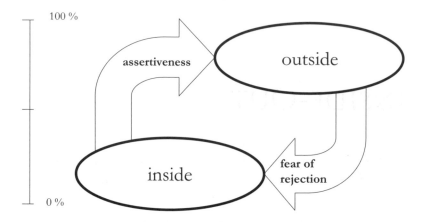

Figure 5.1. How much of your life do you live inside-out vs. outside-in?

do you live your life? Are you constantly worried about or thinking about what others will say? Whether your mother will approve? Whether God will approve? Whether the boss will approve? Whether "polite" company would approve? Do you worry about being judged by others? Do you concern yourself with "appropriate" behavior? Where, on average, would you put yourself on this scale?

For a number of years, we taught a series of executive education programs for a group of executives from Bahrain. One day, we had 55 or so Bahrainis in the classroom, 53 men and two women. And they were telling me that Bahrain was the most open-minded, cosmopolitan country in the Middle East. I allowed as how this was wonderful and then I asked a fellow sitting on the back row:

"Excuse me, Mohamed, I notice that you have black hair."

"I do."

"I wonder, would you be willing to come in tomorrow, cosmopolitan, internationally savvy executive that you are, with platinum blond hair?"

He about fell out of his seat. He was flabbergasted.

"Of course not! Never!"

"Hmm. Why not?"

He'd never been asked this question or such a question and it took him a minute to collect his thoughts. And then he said,

"Men don't do that."

He didn't say "Bahraini men" or "Muslim men." He said, "Men don't do that." It's a semi-conscious assumption about the way the world is or should be.

"Well, wait a minute," I said. "I have four children, a boy and three girls and the girls change their hair color almost weekly. What's the big deal?"

Again, he'd never really thought about this, so he paused, collected his thoughts, and then said,

"I'd be shunned."

And there it was. Living outside in. His assessment of this relatively superficial issue, hair color, was being determined by his peer group. We know, of course, that one's reference group or peer group is a very powerful influence on us. Peer pressure it is thought is even more powerful among teenagers than their parents' influence. Is it in those plastic years that we learn to live outside-in, when the opinions and evaluations of our friends mean so much to us?

I relate this incident to illustrate how common and semi-conscious our tendency to live outside-in can be and is. There are so many things we "should" do to fit into society that many if not most of us learn to pay careful attention to what's acceptable and what's not. In the effort, though, to be a good member, a good citizen, a good student, and a good employee, most of us seem to give up or yield large portions of our inside-outness. We dress appropriately, speak appropriately, behave politely, and while all of that is, honestly, good, we then allow the tendency to spill over into other aspects of our lives like our thinking and our speaking.

The second question related to this diagram is, "Where should one be on this scale to become a leader?" While that might be a question for a leadership class, the relationship here is if one wants to lead one's self, where should one's average be on the scale? I assert that unless we are above fifty percent, we will be spending most of our lives responding to others. And, on average, be living outside-in. The world needs lots of followers, it's true. We also need more leaders. What Doug's discussion of success shows is that most of us, for very fundamental things like what does it mean to be a success in life rely on the opinions and evaluations of others. When Doug's subject says he was living the American dream but not his dream, he's reflecting this outside-in perspective.

The outside-in is essential to society AND doubly dangerous. First, allowing society to define success does not leave room for individual differences. The societal definition of success usually has to do with the accumulation of power and/or wealth. Research done by Driver and Brousseau almost three decades ago suggest that this only one of at least four different naturally occurring success paths. They called this promotion oriented career path the Linear path. See Figure 5.2.

It turns out that there are large numbers of people who *choose* a career path like the one shown in Figure 5.3. These "steady state experts" choose to do the same thing over and over again throughout their careers because they love what they do. Their definition of success has to do with becoming artisans or craftsmen. When I ask executive education groups if they've ever seen a very competent steady state expert ruined by promotion into management every hand in the room goes up. It's a common phenomenon.

So why would a steady state expert be asked to take a linear, managerial job and further, why would they accept? They are asked because most managers assume others have the same assumptions that they do, namely that "success means moving up." They accept either because they don't know themselves well or they too believe that success means moving up.

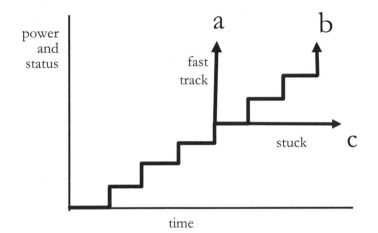

Figure 5.2. Linear success path

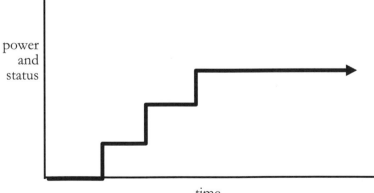

Figure 5.3. Steady state expert success path

Sooner or later they may realize as Doug pointed out in the previous chapter that their lives don't feel very good. And often they fail themselves and their companies in expensive ways.

There are two other voluntarily chosen career paths, Spirals and Transitories. Spirals focus on learning and unlike Linears will give up power and status periodically in order to learn new things. When they get 80 percent of the way to the top, they get bored with the "sameness" of it, and look for a new program, project, industry, company, job or degree. Transitories on the other hand are focused on something other than work. For them, work is a means to get funds to go do what they'd really rather be doing.

In most organizations, the Linears get to the top, and the Linears design the reward systems. That means that Steady State Experts, Spirals, and Transitories working in a linear organization often feel like second-class citizens. They feel undervalued, under-appreciated, and unaccepted for who they are deep inside. In that environment, many begin to suppress how they feel and to conform. They begin to live outside-in and to accept the common model of success swirling about them.

It takes a lot of courage to swim upstream against this current. It takes courage to say to a Linear supervisor, "You know, I really appreciate your confidence in me, but I know myself well enough to know that I'd much rather be doing the work than supervising it. I might be able to do that, but I'd be giving up a big part of who I am and how I want to feel. I hope you'll continue to reward my excellence in what I do, even if not at the same level you would if I took this managerial job. But I want to stay where I am. Thank you."

Most people follow Doug's "success" ladder, the predictable pattern, and are in danger of focusing so much on the *milestones* that they forget how they want to live in between. They are the ones who worry about building their resumes rather than about engaging in what they do. They begin to pay more and more attention to what others expect of them and less and less to what they feel inside. They build their resume line items, and unfortunately along the way may forget how to mobilize their energy and resources in the activities that resonate with them most. They learn, outside-in, to do good enough, to agree, to comply, and go along.

They *see* what's necessary for world-class performance around them because there are role models in almost every organization of those who are clearly deeply passionate about what they do and enjoying every minute of it. They wonder why they don't have as much energy.

Vijay Singh, the professional golfer cited at the beginning of this chapter, also once said that confidence comes from practice and not from winning. Confidence comes from practice, and confidence leads to winning. Singh is known on the PGA tour as a hard worker. He puts in hours and hours of practice. More than most of his peers. He has done this for twenty years. Most amateurs, who "love" the game, don't put in anywhere near the kind of practice that Singh does. Why?

WILLIAM JAMES

THE IDEA TO BE CONSENTED TO MUST BE
KEPT FROM FLICKERING AND GOING OUT.
IT MUST BE HELD STEADILY BEFORE THE
MIND UNTIL IT FILLS THE MIND. THE IDEA
MUST BE GIVEN A QUIET HEARING.

Informed Energy

Informed Energy

*T*here are many reasons people who love doing something do not put in the time to get better. Most reasons are very personal and often misunderstood.

My experience with the world-class performers I interviewed and those people I consult with who are stuck in their lives provide me clear data about the difference.

As I listened to several hundred people I interviewed, it occurred to me they had a fundamentally different definition of performance than any I had heard before — and they had something in common with one another although most of them had never met one another.

Using their own words the consistently conveyed, "Performance is the creation and expression of an idea." Then they said their work was to hold that idea for long enough for it to inform their actions.

William James, over a century ago, said the same sort of thing. He believed that it is possible only for a strong willed person:

> *"... who hears the small voice unflinchingly, and who, when the death-bringing consideration comes, looks at its face, consents to its presence, clings to it, affirms it, and holds it fast, in spite of the host of exciting mental images which rise in revolt against it and would expel it from the mind."*

The difference between Vijay Singh and my neighbor who loves playing golf on weekends is simply the difference in their ideas of what golf is — or how much it is a part of ourselves.

Have you ever interrupted somebody who said, "Don't bother me, I'm working?" The world-class performers I interviewed almost never used those terms. They were answering a call, a whisper they felt compelled to express. For them *work* is a noun, not a verb and never a place. Expressing their idea into the world is their work. The idea is so big it leaves little room for distraction from other ideas or anything disconnected from this big idea.

They gave these ideas "a quiet hearing." They explored it. Unbundled it. Listened to it. They connected the rest of their lives to it. The more they listen to it, the bigger the idea grows. They develop the skills needed to express it. They are full of wonder. They play with it. The more the idea fits their skills, the more the idea can be expressed in the real world, the bigger the idea grows.

This takes a level of trust, a level of discipline, a level of risk. These performers were never afraid to pursue their big idea even when it meant risking the loss of other experiences or even going against what others said.

In my consulting life, I have been fortunate enough to watch open-heart surgery, spend the night on an aircraft carrier, train with a world-class tri-athlete, run pass patterns for an NFL quarterback, sit in on recording sessions of Grammy award-winning musicians. In other words, I've been behind the scenes. I've been there when no one else is watching and what I learned amazed me.

The hours I spent in those situations fascinated me because I was so curious what makes people great at what they do and because these are the kind of people you want to spend time with.

The detail it takes to be great, to be world-class, in any of these areas, however — doing what they do day after day — simply did not hold my attention. I was constantly distracted by fear, worry, and doubt.

I didn't share their dream, their idea. Without it, I was simply exhausted. I simply couldn't inform my energy or release it into doing the necessary work.

While the people I interviewed experienced the same exhaustion, their idea was simply too strong to let go of. In fact, the act of getting better, of improving, of learning, of practicing actually alleviated their distractions because it became their focus alone.

Most of all, their ideas grew into dreams the more time and effort they put forth, gave them energy, informed their energy into doing more work. Many of them said it was like playing as a kid, stopping only when someone they cared about "called them home for dinner." Many of them described themselves as kids with the skills and knowledge of adults.

Some of the people I interviewed were world-class at several different things. They told me that what they learned from their first idea was that which made them successful, what turned an idea into a dream was how they felt doing the work. When they finished one career, they used those criteria to find their next idea.

That is when I came to understand that the dream had as much to do with energy and feel as anything else. When one career ended, they wanted to find a new idea based on how it made them feel, a feel that made the work more like play, more fulfilling and sustainable, than how the rest of us might choose an idea.

I have come to view this as *informed energy*. The level of detail required to be world-class demands that the energy we have be put to good use, to do meaningful work. In physics, physical work is done by energy, but the energy must know what to do. World-class ideas require useful information free from distractions competing for our attention and informed energy increases the likelihood we will pay attention to our idea.

Many a weekend golfer who loves golf has an idea that has not become a dream. If someone told you they loved you, but only showed up on occasional weekends unprepared to be with you, would you believe they love you? Probably not.

What I learned from these world-class performers about love is that love is what you do. Love is what you feel when you do the work that fits you. Love is the expression of an idea. To the outside world, it might look like work, but inside it feels like love, a love so big they rarely turn away from the idea, an idea they've nurtured into a dream.

WARREN BUFFET

CHAINS OF HABIT ARE TOO LIGHT TO BE FELT
UNTIL THEY ARE TOO HEAVY TO BE BROKEN.

HABITS

*D*oes how you think inform your energy? People tend to be creatures of habit. Over the last four years I have been privileged to travel to most continents around the globe conducting executive education leadership development seminars. In these seminars I ask people a series of questions that point out the difficulty in getting people to change what they do.

For example, let me ask at whatever age you have now attained in life, consider all of the people whom you have met thus far. If you consider their visible behavior, what they say and do that you could capture on film, what I will call Level 1, what proportion, on average, of their visible behavior, would you guesstimate to be habitual, that is, unthinkingly repetitive?

Write your answer here:

The answer that a thousand executives, country managers, functional managers, and marketing managers worldwide will say is about 75 percent.

The second question is, "Consider all the people that you've met thus far in life with regard to what I will call Level 2, conscious thought. That is, given all the people whom you've met thus far in life, what proportion of *the way they think* would you guesstimate to be habitual?"

Write your answer here:

Managers worldwide will say, on average, 85 percent.

Let's consider now what I will call Level 3, the semi-conscious or subconscious core Values, Assumptions, Beliefs, and Expectations we have about the way the world is or should be. We can call these "VABEs" for short. Now, consider all the people whom you've met thus far in life and write down your guesstimate of the proportion of their values, assumptions, beliefs, and expectations about the way the world is or should be that are habitual.

Write your estimate here:

The managers I mentioned above will typically say 95 or 99 percent.

If these numbers seem high to you, consider how reluctant various groups all over the world have been to change. Look at Northern Ireland, the former Yugoslavia, the Middle East, Lebanon, Rwanda and Burundi, you pick your part of the world and consider how long dysfunctional conflicts have been persisting all over the globe. When I say dysfunctional, I mean that these conflicts add no value in the future growth development evolution and enhancement of the human race. Christians have been fighting about various points of doctrine for centuries. Muslims have been fighting about various points of doctrine for centuries. Sometimes the issues are related to race, sometimes to religion, sometimes to economic status, sometimes to alma mater, and sometimes simply to where you were born. I call these "functionally irrelevant differences."

We can contrast these with "functionally relevant differences" that have to do with issues like skill, knowledge, energy, and performance. A person's religion, race, gender, ethnic origin, and place of birth, often have very little if anything to do *directly* with a person's ability to perform. Education, effort, skill development, curiosity, and interestingly the ability to manage how one feels, all have direct implications for a person's ability to perform.

So when we begin to think about teaching someone, leading someone, or influencing someone, we confront immediately this issue of habituality. While it's true that people *can* change, and most human beings argue that they can change, the reality seems to be that most people do not change.

When we are tiny children, we are utterly dependent on our parents for our well-being. We cannot roll over by ourselves, we cannot change ourselves, we cannot feed ourselves, we cannot protect ourselves from outside forces. Then when we grow older, we get bigger, we get smarter; we become more independent in some ways. But the question lingers. Will we ever be able to re-examine the core VABEs that were imprinted on us when we were defenseless children once we become adults?

The most important question in life

Bestselling author, Mihalyi Csikszentmihalyi, poses what I have come to believe is *the* central question in life: Will you ever be anything more than a vessel transmitting the memes (VABEs) and the genes of previous generations on to the next? This is a very important question when it comes to growing up, becoming a mature adult, and becoming an independent professional in a flat interconnected world. It's important because unless we find the time and the ability to re-examine those core VABEs that we were given as children, we will never be anything more than riders on the tips of spears thrown by previous generations, contributing to functionally irrelevant conflicts.

Many people find this a very threatening question. It *is* a threatening question, in the sense that mature adulthood invites a person to re-examine what he or she was taught as a child and make his or her own determination as relatively independent beings, whether or not what they were taught is true and/or functional. This does not

> Will you ever be anything more than a vessel transmitting the memes (VABEs) and genes of previous generations on to the next?

mean, of course, that all of the things we were taught as children are bad. It does mean that, unless we are able to as adults re-examine what we were taught as children, the conflicts in the world are not likely to go away.

Will you ever be anything more than a vessel transmitting the memes (VABEs) and genes of previous generations on to the next?

Should you always clean your plate at dinner? Are people of a different color not to be trusted? Are people who have (or haven't) an education not to be trusted? Should you not dye your hair? Should you always do what an authority figure tells you to do? Should you never pick up strangers? Is counting calories the best way to manage your weight? Is there a God? Is there life after death? Should we continue trying to take revenge on the people who live in the next valley over?

These are just a few examples of questions that we need to begin to bring under examination if we want to live in a peaceful world. If we don't deal with these questions, the conflicts in the world will continue as they are. If we learn individually and in groups and as cultures and as nations to re-examine the assumptions we've made or that were handed to us from previous generations, perhaps we have a chance of accelerating our growth toward a more peaceful interrelated collaborative world.

One of the most important assumptions that we've already introduced is "that professionals will do what they have to do regardless of how they feel." This assumption, as we have already discussed, prevents people from performing at their best. One way to assert one's mature adulthood is to become clear on what it is that you want and to include, in that definition, a definition of how you want to *feel* in addition to what you want to have and what you want to do and what you want to experience. One of the most surprisingly confusing question seems to be, "What do you want?" Could you answer that question? Write your answer in the space below:

For large numbers of people worldwide, it has become habitual to suppress feel, to avoid managing feel, and to view managing *feel* as an irrelevant criterion. What history over the last two centuries has taught us, if nothing else, is that how people feel matters enormously. We learned this in the political arena, and the athletic arena, and in the business arena. On average, how many times a day do you pause to think about or become aware of how you feel? In other words, what's your habitual pattern with regard to attending to and managing how you feel? The odds are, given Doug's research and my consulting practice, most of you pay very little attention to this very important connection to performance. This is a habit that we hope you will consider re-examining and perhaps changing. After all, we are, to a large degree, a collection of habits.

ALFRED NORTH WHITEHEAD

FAMILIAR THINGS HAPPEN, AND MANKIND DOES NOT BOTHER ABOUT THEM. IT REQUIRES A VERY UNUSUAL MIND TO UNDERTAKE THE ANALYSIS OF THE OBVIOUS.

Routines

ROUTINES

$\mathcal{M}$ any of the people I interviewed — from the pro golfer and the pro tennis player to the pilots, the surgeons, and even the CEO — followed routines they created for one specific purpose. Following these routines helps them feel the way they want to feel when it mattered most. In many cases, the use of a routine allows the body and mind to reset, to recalibrate. Routines allow them to focus on something they can control that also prepares them to perform well.

One night I was talking to a woman who was a college All American, a tour pro, and now a successful women's college golf coach who was named National Coach of the Year. We spoke about the benefits of routines, but she also pointed out the danger they could become habitual and mindless. She pointed out that if one does the routine for its own sake, it can become mundane, then the purpose for doing the routine is lost and along with it any hope for an impact on performance.

World-class performers do work and they do what works. When they have habits, those habits center on feeling what is working and dropping what is not. Their habits are more like radars that constantly monitor work and life. They check in with themselves constantly, seeking useful feedback, not judgment.

Those performers I interviewed figured out what fueled their vessel, what nurtured it, what made that vessel want to get out of bed in the morning

and get to work. Maybe it is the people I chose to interview, but most if not all of them "felt" what they were, who they were, and they followed where that *feel* took them. If they had habits and routines, they were organized around that feel, *their feel*. They acted responsibly in the world not allowing their vessel to damage those around them.

After I had done many of these interviews, I read the book *Genome* by Matt Ridley, in which he wonders if there is a gene for free will. Ridley quotes psychologist Lyndon Eaves as saying, "Freedom is the ability to stand up and transcend the limitations of the environment." This captures exactly the sentiment expressed in my interviews time and again. "Freedom lies in expressing your own determinism. It is not the determinism that matters. It is the ownership."

I would add that *world-class* is determined by the work you do with what you own (in terms of your genes and memes).

One CEO I interviewed expressed it this way:

> *"My observation is that despite what the* Declaration of Independence *literally says, all men are not created equal. We're blessed with different sets of skills. That is the truth that is self-evident. It doesn't mean that one person is better than the other, or has greater rights than the other. Jefferson's equality is in the eyes of God and in the eyes of the law. As for the rest of us, no matter how industrious I became, how hard I practiced, I couldn't play basketball the way Michael Jordan plays.*
>
> *The first thing you have to do if you want to perform well is to make sure you pursue a discipline where you have some native abilities and skills. When you focus your energy on something that feels comfortable to you, you know you aren't always swimming upstream.*
>
> *The second thing you have to do, persevere. There are very few people who achieve success or high performance without a lot of perseverance along the way.*

Finally, you have to catch some breaks along the way. Separating success from performance, I think you can perform well in a variety of areas, but it takes a little luck to achieve visible success or financial success. Certainly in athletics it is obvious. I'm a Redskin fan, and every year you see someone get hurt and the next guy steps up. Every time a receiver or running back got hurt on the Skins, the next guy turned out to be as good or better. Those are people who would never have had an opportunity if it were not for the injury to the predecessor.

In the broadest sense choosing an area in which you have some ability, perseverance, and luck are most important to personal success."

While people I interviewed would say it in their own individual way, their descriptions were in a sense a combination of what Ridley and this CEO were saying. Express your own determinism, not someone else's.

As Abraham Lincoln said "Whatever you are, be a good one."

THE RESONANCE MODEL

BILL GATES, *MICROSOFT*

 WHEN PEOPLE GO TO WORK, IT'S IMPORTANT THAT THEY BE CONNECTED TO A DREAM.

Dreams

DREAMS

*B*e a good one. How does feel relate to being good at something? When I visited Doug's lecture that first night, and he asked how did I want to feel, I couldn't answer the question. No one, not my mother, not my father, none of my teachers or employers have ever asked me that question. I couldn't sleep that night. It took me, in fact, eighteen months and about 40 drafts to come up with what I thought was a for-the-moment satisfactory answer: light, unhurried and engaged.

I got that after tearing my right rotator cuff playing basketball. I had the surgery, but still had a full professional slate including two professional conference talks in California, one in the LA area and one in San Francisco. So ten days after surgery with the staples still in, I flew to LA. My wife came along to help me up and down and to help shlep the bags. The LA talk went fine, to a packed house actually. Then we rented a car and drove up Highway 1 to San Francisco. We played word games along the way to pass the time and enjoyed the beauty of scenic California. We visited Susan's brother in Atascadero and then drove up to the City.

I was unaware of how, if at all, my body was compensating for the staples, the sling, and the cuts by hunching and leaning. We arrived at the hotel, parked in the underground lot, pulled our wheelies into the hallway, up the elevator and into the room. Susan was in the bathroom and I bent over to take off my shoes, one-handed, and as I did, I felt every vertebra in my back go "pop, pop, pop, pop, pop" all the way up as my back muscles seized harshly. It was excruciating. I cried out and was immediately in a fetal ball on the bed.

We were supposed to go out that night with my mentor, Tony Athos, a man whose initials are tattooed on my wrist. I couldn't move. Susan undressed me, fed me Advil, and tucked me in, still in the fetal ball. Tony brought Chinese in and we talked about how absurd this all was. It was also the day we were supposed to take the staples out. Susan had the tool, and so with Tony supervising, she pulled the 23 staples from my shoulder.

The next day the hotel rented a portable elevator (they have such things), Susan dressed me, we got a wheelchair, and I was wheeled downstairs and up onto the stage, still unable to stand at all. I was sitting there in front of a thousand people, looking at my wheel-chaired image on the fifteen foot screens spread throughout the audience, thinking, "there's something wrong with this picture."

I liked being on stage, I liked giving talks, I liked in some small way helping people find themselves through my teaching, writing, and professional activities. Sitting in a wheelchair, staring into the glare of the lights, I knew this was wrong.

We had to cancel the rest of our post-work vacation and wheel me home. I learned for the first time about the handicapped world and the paths one has to take to travel in it. It's inconvenient, inefficient, time consuming, and left me with a sadness born of dependency.

Finally home, I cleared my calendar for the next six months. Canceled all my appointments. Susan had a lot to do with that. She scolded me for not slowing down, for not paying attention to my body, for not, basically paying attention to how I felt. I had fifty years of experience focusing on what I did. I believed that what you love is what you do. I remember my mom's voice teaching me, sternly sometimes, "You do the job. You do the job right. It doesn't matter how you feel. Just do the job." Push through. You can conquer pain, sleeplessness, fatigue, boredom, anger, depression, anything. Just push through.

I discovered there are limits. It's poignant for me writing this. I'm on an airplane on a 15 hour trip from Dubai to the U.S. Last year, I tore my left rotator cuff in taekwondo, holding a large pad (improperly it turns out) for a flying, jumping, kicking ten-year-old. My shoulder hurts like hell every day now. I've slept for eight hours already (unusual for me on planes), and I'm "awake." I could nap more, but I'm awake and I owe Doug and the process this chapter. Besides, I like writing. I'm describing this event from ten years ago and in some ways, habitually, reliving it live.

Anyway, I cleared my calendar and worked on the third edition of my book, *Level Three Leadership*. The book just tumbled out of me. Every day, I awoke, did my rehab and exercise, wrote, and rested. My back released. My mind released. I felt calm and peaceful, but alive and engaged. Looking back on that experience six months later, I realized that THAT was it. *Light, unhurried and engaged.*

When I over commit as I'm wont to do I feel heavy. I tend to stress and eat more and get heavy. When I over commit, I get hurried and feel like a chicken with my head cut off running around in circles. Yet lying on the couch eating chips and watching TV doesn't do it for me. I love this feeling of being light, unhurried, and engaged. More and more, I've realized now, I also like to be connected to others, not just alone in my "productivity."

SO, light, unhurried, engaged and connected. That's how I want to feel. The definition did not come easy. The implementation even less so. I had 50 years of habits teaching me physically, emotionally, and intellectually to do more, to produce, to be "results-oriented." It IS, after all, a "results-oriented" world. Thing is, when I focus *first* on "light, unhurried, engaged, and connected" I produce more and with much higher quality. High performance begins with an internal dream. See Figure 9.1.

Focusing on feel has required an intentional, inside-out effort to manage my habits and tendencies. Some of those are genetic — I come from four generations of alcoholics and I have a tendency to obsess a little. So, I've printed my "internal life's dream," how I want to feel, on my checks. Every time I write a check it reminds me to focus on *feel* first. I sometimes post it in my bathroom on the mirror, to remind me, think about *feel* first and the to-do list later.

This effort has had a profound effect on my life. I'm much more cheerful, much more upbeat, much more "in control" of my life than I was before. Sure, I have relapses, and days go by when I forget. More and more I think about how I want to feel and manage my days to suit. I've come to feel I'm living my life, not some mythical life that someone else — mom, dad, god, dean, client — wants me to live.

It may seem odd, but I had a moment of pride just this past week. I'd given a two-day seminar. This requires me to facilitate, guide, and sustain high energy for a room full of 50 people for eight hours a day. Usually by

dream

how to you want to feel?

Figure 9.1. High performance begins with an internal dream

the end of the day, I need to rest. On this day, the seminar went really well. Our hosts decided last minute contrary to previous plans to have a dinner that night in my honor. They'd also arranged a tour of their local facilities. The tour began immediately after the graduation exercises. I was exhausted. My knees were beginning to hurt more and more (from the bi-lateral quadriceps tendon ruptures I'd suffered a year ago), and I could hardly stay awake. The tour was to last 30 minutes. It took us an hour just to get to the plant. It was pitch black and you couldn't see anything. My host didn't want to drive back into town and then home an hour each way, so he transferred me into another car with a driver who barely spoke English and sent me on my way. An hour later, not quite yet to the hotel, I was a basket case and my knees hurt like crazy.

The old me would have ignored all of this, sucked it up and gone out to dinner 20 minutes later. Instead, I took a huge risk. I called my contact and apologized and begged off for the night. I'm sure when she got to the dinner that the sponsors were annoyed, even irked, perhaps angry. I went to my room, had a light room service meal and went to bed. I was managing how I felt, something that for decades I did not do. The next morning, I felt much better. I had a good day. It was an example of my progress in managing life and performance. I was living my dream more than I had been.

Doug's interviewees have described many different what I call "internal life's dreams," how they wanted to feel. (See Figure 9.1.) Most people think about an "external life's dream," the thing you can put on your resume or point to as what you do. Doug has this odd way of describing the difference: he says "Resonance is like peeing your pants. Everyone can see it, but only you can feel it." "Gross," I thought the first time he said that. Later, as usual, I thought more about it, and yup, he's right. Only you can feel it. If you have the right *feel*, you do better.

Doug's subjects describe "easy speed" (Olympic gold medalist swimmer), and "playing to win against the world's best competition" (Olympic gold medalist basketball player). I've asked a lot of people Doug's question, "How do you want to feel?" and only a very, very few can answer it right off. Our dean for example, a renowned teacher, said immediately, "Buoyant, connected mastery." Then he went on to describe all three terms as what he seeks and often gets in the classroom. A rising tide of energy, everyone is in touch with each other, and yet, in the midst of the distributed communication, he's in charge.

How do *you* want to feel? What's your internal life's dream? Can you write your first draft here?

What Doug will tell you, though, is that it takes more than *seeing* it to create or recreate your internal dream. It takes intense preparation. His chapter on informed idea energy makes the point. If you don't love a thing enough to persist despite what the outside world is saying, you won't have enough energy to practice, prepare, rehearse to get really good. Really, really, world-class good.

CHARLES LINDBERGH

BUILDING AN AIRPLANE IS EASIER THAN
THE EVOLUTIONARY PROCESS OF THE
FLIGHT OF A BIRD. I'D RATHER BE AROUND
BIRDS.

Preparation

PREPARATION

*T*he most critical and consistent preparation world-class performers do is probably not what you imagine. It involves feeling their energy, setting it in motion — what I call *informing it* — through practice and ongoing learning, testing that energy privately and publicly, and protecting it.

When they inform their energy properly, because they are pursuing their dream from the inside-out, they experience *resonance*. When what's inside resonates with the world around them, their energy increases, focus sharpens, skills flow. The process looks something like the following:

dream
how do you want/need to feel?

**revisit
the dream**
how do you get it
back?

preparation
what makes that happen?

obstacles
what gets in the way
or takes it away?

Figure 10.1. Resonance

Other people have written about *flow* and *resonant leadership*, but they frequently describe these terms as results of achievement as in, "I achieved flow."

Resonance, as I mean it, is a process, not a result nor a technique. Results are part of the process and results can give the process its meaning. Resonance amplifies energy in us the same way a tuning fork does in music and physics. And how do we experience energy? We feel it. How these performers feel informs their energy into a responsible dream they set out to fulfill.

I call what I heard in interviews *resonance* because of something Joseph Campbell said in the *Power of Myth*:

> *I think that what we're seeking is an experience of being alive, so that our life experiences on the purely physical plane will have resonances with our own innermost being and reality so that we actually feel the rapture of being alive.*

Many of us grow up believing that paying attention to how we feel is irresponsible or selfish. Yet, in my research I heard from those around these world-class performers that they made the people around them better because they understood that how everyone *felt* mattered, that each person needed his or her own dream, a dream informed by feel, energy informed into meaningful work, movement or growth.

Their reward was not the result of a dream deferred or keeping themselves hidden away from view, waiting to be released once they were successful in the eyes of society.

As Richard Feynman said:

> *"Someone said I must have been thrilled about winning the Nobel Prize. I told him I really didn't care about it. I remember when I got invited to join some group in college that everyone wanted to belong to. I joined and all we did in our meetings was to sit*

around and judge how others might be worthy to be in our group. I hated it so I quit. When I won the Nobel Prize, sure, it felt good, but to some degree, it was the same thing. What do I care what five guys sitting in a room somewhere in Sweden thought about me. I already had my reward. For me, the true pleasure is in finding the thing out."

Preparation means preparing to live your dream, not simply achieving one.

The performers I interviewed were very detailed in how they prepared. A World Champion Archer built an indoor target area next to his house so he could shoot whenever he wanted. A musician built a studio at his house so he could capture his music even when he awoke at four in the morning with a song in his head. A CEO in bioengineering designed his office so he felt the way he wanted to feel there. A heart surgeon chose music to listen to at crucial times of an operation, knowing exactly what songs he wanted to hear during the most intense times of the surgery. Another CEO made sure he had family time each night and each morning even if he had more work to do, adjusting his sleep schedule not out of obligation, but to enjoy his family.

When I help someone redefine work, we go into great detail. Often the details they have never reflected on and some parts of how they feel are missing so I send them off to re-experience their lives, and collect data. I want them to see that as disciplined as they might believe they were, they are missing some critical data, the data of feel. What has been informing their energy that they never noticed before?

Once we have that data, we put it to work. The more you feel your world, your life, the more data you have, the better decisions you will make. *Feel* is a skill, a gift from nature. Without the data feel provides us, we return to the past. Our energy is informed by past memories of feel, often from when we were kids. We return to someone else's definition of work as something outside of us. We return to the need for approval or the fear of rejection.

Preparation for living your dream is ongoing, revisited again and again. Prepare to learning what informs your energy by paying attention to how your life feels. Collect that data and then use it. If doing certain things make you feel the way you want to feel, if you find you get work done more powerfully when you feel a certain way, structure your environment around that information.

Let me give you how this works in my work.

When I consult with groups, I ask, "How would you describe a great team?"

The answers I get are predictable — energized, a buzz, passionate, connected, supported, good communication, a common purpose, everyone knows their role.

Almost no one ever says, "strategically sound," "well funded," "great products."

People instinctively know that being on a great team has a feel to it, a feel that fits their mission. They get it.

I then ask the same people, "How do you prepare to be this great team?"

Amazingly, they get off track in an instant. They start describing a winning spirit, goals, rewards, and a long list outside of themselves.

No one has ever asked them how they feel or even how they want to feel. The people in the group have never asked one another. Many people assume we only feel the way a great team feels when we win, when we achieve. Yet how often do we see it happen that someone becomes successful externally, someone who made it to the top, only to start falling backwards right away?

World-class performers prepare to live their dream, to feel the way they wanted to feel when it mattered most by feeling it when it seemed to matter least. When they work together, they are asking themselves and asking each other about the feel of work itself.

The CEO walks the aisles of a grocery store to understand the marketing techniques of successful brands. The Olympic swimmer plays with the water at his local YMCA. The surgeon darns socks because he liked working with his hands. The mechanical engineer works on his car because he loves solving puzzles. Einstein sat in a room drawing diagrams because he wondered about the world.

This is the keys that made these people different. They felt the way they wanted to feel almost every day because they loved it and, they would come to find out, that it allowed them to feel that way when it mattered most. Every presentation, every sales call, every meeting was a chance for them to live their dream if even on a small scale. The heart surgeon listened to the same music during routine bypass surgeries allowing him to control his internal environment during the truly difficult cases. The CEO developed relationships with his employees, relationships he came to rely on when he had difficult news to share, when he had to ask more.

In other words, they got where they were by living the dream, connecting with people, learning about themselves and others, collecting data about how they felt and wanted to feel. They loved doing that minute by minute. When they were under pressure, they knew how to revisit the feeling they needed to get through.

Too often I run into people who practice a lot but it is not anything more than going through motions of simply working on a skill. They feel good when they are done and congratulated themselves approval for their effort, but this practice does not prepare them for performing in the real world. They taught their minds and bodies to perform a skill over and over again. Yet they did not prepare themselves to do those same skills under pressure, when it mattered. The variation and energy isn't there. They may even become bored.

As often as they can, world-class performers seek out preparation in ways that allow them to feel how they want to feel. They create the environments in which they will perform as best as they can. Great speakers know how they want a room to feel to them. They go in early and get to know the people before they speak so they can connect with them and speak to them as individuals.

When we have little control over the environment, when the challenge is greater, we rely on those things we can create in ourselves. We must depend on and take responsibility for how we feel.

The musician who built a studio at his house also took responsibility for how he felt on one of the biggest stages in the world. As he played the National Anthem at a NBA All Star Game he noticed his hands were shaking. For a moment, he had no idea what to do. He decided to simply put his hands on the keys and start playing. As he felt the keys, he felt connected to what he loved and off he went.

When an Olympic swimmer poised for his start in the 1996 Olympics, he said it felt like practice. What he meant by that was he felt what he wanted to feel, what he'd felt a hundred times in his pool. He swam with what he called *easy speed* and won the Gold, but only after several years of preparing to feel easy speed, something he had not prepared for four years earlier when he settled for Silver.

What keys will you put your hands on? How will you prepare for easy speed during your important sales call, presentation, meeting? How do you want to feel when what matters to you matters the most? How will you make that feel happen? Feel is a skill. Practice and prepare. Collect your data and put them to work.

TOM WEISKOPF

I REMEMBER EXACTLY THE DAY I STOPPED ENJOYING GOLF. IT WAS THE DAY I TURNED PRO.

Obligation

OBLIGATION

*P*ractice and prepare. Does one do that from choice or from obligation? Obligation is an outside-in process; that is, when you feel duty or obligation, it came, in the first instance, from the outside. You never *have* to do anything unless you were told at one point by someone else to do so. You may have internalized those thoughts and they may have become semi- or sub-conscious values or assumptions or beliefs for you, but in the first instance, they came from somewhere else. In the end, it's very hard if not impossible to get world-class out of duty or obligation.

Obligation is a two-edged sword. On the one hand, it can be the genesis of some good things. In the business world and even in the athletic world and other "worlds" obligation can be a foundation for mediocrity. Consider this question which I've asked thousands of managers in executive education and consulting settings: "What happens when a person goes from the land of choice into the land of obligation? What happens to energy level — up, flat or down? What about productivity? Engagement? Learning? Investment? Innovation? Creativity?" You pick your dimension. Most people readily acknowledge that when a person goes from choice to obligation, all of these indicators go down. Consider the diagram in Figure 11.1.

This should not be surprising since the concept of individual choice and freedom is the basis for democracy. People want to choose what they

do and what they spend their time on. When that freedom is removed, people lose energy and enter into an obligatory mindset, or what we might call a "duty cycle." See Figure 11.2.

The problem is that obligation is an inherently energy-draining mental process. Consider the comment by Dave Scott, at 49 years of age, the six-

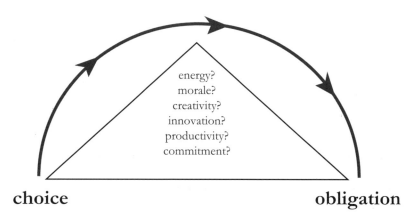

energy?
morale?
creativity?
innovation?
productivity?
commitment?

choice   **obligation**

Figure 11.1. What happens when you go from choice to obligation?

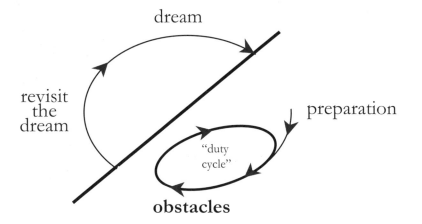

dream

revisit
the
dream

preparation

"duty
cycle"

obstacles

Figure 11.2. The obligatory duty cycle

time winner of the Hawaii Ironman Triathlon. This is a race composed of three segments, a 2.2-mile swim in the open sea, a 112-mile bicycle race, and a 26.2-mile marathon run, back to back to back. "During a race, I never wear a wristwatch, and my bike doesn't have a speedometer. They're distractions. All I work on is finding a rhythm that feels strong and sticking to it."[1]

Wait a minute. The vast majority of the world's competitors don't do it that way. They carry a watch, they watch for the milestones, and they calculate. If they're behind, they say to themselves, "I have to pick it up." And by so doing they put themselves in an obligatory mindset, and that obligation causes tension and drains energy. The Olympic swimmer Doug described previously did the same thing when he acceded to the outside-in pressures of the media to focus on winning instead of how he wanted to feel.

But Scott says the watch and speedometer are *distractions*. He focuses on how he wants to feel, puts his mind there, finds a good rhythm and then just focuses on that feel. By the way, he's blowing everyone else away.

Clearly, if he hadn't practiced and prepared, he couldn't win. The point is that focusing on winning puts one in an obligatory mindset and counter-productively and ironically drains energy needed to compete at the world-class level.

Consider this question: What's your dominant thought on the way into work on a typical work day? Wait a minute. Think about it. Pick a day. Any day. What's the most common thought you have while on your way into work?

---

[1]*Outside*, 9/03, p. 122

Most people will say, "What do I *have* to do today?" We hear this all over the world. Note that this is an obligatory mindset. You've *put* yourself into a mental state of obligation, and just like those racers working against Dave Scott, you've put yourself one down to begin with. It's a habit, a mental habit that drains energy.

At this point, many business people will argue that they or their companies are asking people to do things they otherwise would never do. Who wants to be a coal miner? Or an automobile assembler? Or a welder? In my experience, there are a lot of people who do. And a lot who don't. But if you start your business and your management philosophy with the notion that "nobody wants to do these jobs, so we have to pay people so they feel obligated to do them," I'd say you're beginning with a philosophy that soon will be focused on "how can I motivate my people?"

The first answer is to stop taking choice away from them. Let them make more choices about how they work. The more rules you have in order to maintain more control, the less energy and less engagement you're likely to have. Choice is inherently energizing while obligation is inherently de-energizing. Sustainable energy is necessary to practice and prepare for world-class performance and to overcome obstacles that crop up in your way.

HELEN KELLER

WHEN ONE DOOR OF HAPPINESS CLOSES,
ANOTHER OPENS; BUT OFTEN WE LOOK SO
LONG AT THE CLOSED DOOR THAT WE DO
NOT SEE THE ONE WHICH HAS OPENED FOR
US.

Obstacles

OBSTACLES

One day I happened to be sitting in the audience, an audience full of surgeons, when Jim told the story of Ironman Dave Scott. Sitting in front of me were what I will call "old school" surgeons. When Jim presented Scott's strategy, one of them leaned in toward the other and whispered, "So I guess that must work for everybody" and they both laughed. They didn't get it, did not understand what Jim was saying, and I suspect they never would.

The fact that Dave Scott did not use a watch or set goals was not the ultimate point. Dave Scott figured out what worked for him. He did not confuse technique with skill. World-class performers like Dave Scott do what works for them. Period.

The success ladder I showed earlier is made up of goals (get good grades, get into a good college, etc.) and a narrow path up the ladder showing the path to achievement. World-class performers rarely take a narrow path. They often blaze a trail where none exists. They step outside the narrow, outside-in defined path to success. Consequently, they find ways around obstacles that stop the rest of us. They create a wider path with more freedom, more choices, more creativity.

While a focused dream can be useful, having a narrow path to that dream can kill the dream.

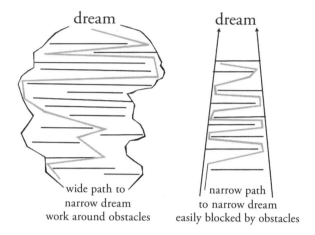

dream   dream

wide path to   narrow path
narrow dream   to narrow dream
work around obstacles easily blocked by obstacles

Figure 12.1. Dream Path

Remember that a dream is how you want to feel — a feel you are willing to live, to pursue, to sacrifice for, to work for. One successful businessman I worked with said I had defined happiness. Happiness he said is feeling the way you want to feel.

If you live outside in, then the dream might appear as something outside of you, achieved by some well-defined path. Other times, we find the greatest obstacles to our dream inside of us.

I could make a list of the reasons we could not live our dreams — money, talent, circumstances, and so on, but those reasons demonstrate outside-in thinking. If a dream is defined by how we feel, then maybe the real obstacle to our dreams is our inability to feel, or an underdeveloped sense of feel.

Think about it, or rather *feel* about it. What defines the dream for most people is how they feel, not a solution to an intellectual challenge. We use feel to find and pursue our dreams. It is how we make sense of what attracts us, what nurtures an idea into a dream, seeking out and renewing the energy needed to perform a dream's work.

If we do not feel, can we really say we dream in a useful way? If we do not feel, how do we find our dream? How do we feel what we never touch?

I learned from the people I interviewed that our greatest obstacle and therefore our greatest challenge is found in our own *response*. Fear, envy, jealousy, judgment, timidity, anger, frustration. Show me someone pursuing his or her dream and I will show you every one of these responses to be obstacles.

World-class performers respond differently to outside circumstances and also their own responses. When something happens that blocks their path, the trail they are blazing in the world around them, at first they respond just like the rest of us. They feel fear, worry, doubt. They might even respond to success with hubris and overconfidence that brings them down. Instead of *expressing* those responses, though, instead of lashing out at the world and those around them, they respond to their initial response: they respond to response.

Several of the people I interviewed called this alternative response the ultimate competition, a place in each of us where our skills fall short of our vision, of our dream, and yet they find a way through when it matters most.

Take for example Olympic Gold Medalist Jeff Rouse. He was the world record holder in the 100 meter backstroke and went into the Barcelona Olympics as the heavy favorite. A few days before his race, he boarded a school bus with other athletes to commute from the Olympic Village to the pool where he would work out.

The bus was cramped, hot, and slow. Rouse was miserable. The bus got lost and what should have been a ten minute ride took forty-five minutes. On top of all that, the bus dropped them at the bottom of a hill, a half a mile climb to the pool.

Rouse got inside the stadium, still stewing, grabbed a mat to stretch out, to get loose, and slammed it on the ground next to the swimmer who represented the greatest threat to Rouse's pursuit of Gold.

As he stretched, he grumbled about the miserable bus ride and how the uphill climb tired out his legs during the days leading up to competition swimmers exert as little energy as possible. He complained. He whined.

Mark Tewksbury took it all in and for the first time realized Rouse was just like him. More important he realized, Rouse could be beaten.

In fact, Tewksbury won the Gold. He then went on to write a book about his Olympic experience and he dedicated a chapter to that moment when Rouse gave in to his misery.

When I met Rouse soon after this and as we worked together, as he prepared for the Atlanta Olympics, we addressed this head on. He realized his mistake. He had given into his initial response to an inconvenience and in so doing likely opened the door for Tewksbury.

As the Atlanta Olympics approached, I asked Rouse what he would do if a similar situation occurred. Neither one of us believed it would not bother Rouse or that he could talk himself out of his response. We did not believe he would think himself out of it.

We agreed, however, that he could *feel* his way out of it, and the place he felt best was in the water. If he had it to do over again, if he had the choice, he would jump into the pool and play with the water, to feel the way he wanted to feel. He would respond to his own response — to the misery, to the fear, to anger — before he would start his preparation, his routine.

Rouse is not alone. I've heard countless examples of similar situations in my work. A surgeon losing an elderly patient in the morning only to have the same operation scheduled on another grandparent later that day. A salesman fumbles a presentation to a minor client in the morning knowing he has the same presentation to a major client after lunch.

In each case, a response of worry or doubt, maybe even fear, will not improve the situation. They needed to respond to their own responses before responding to the situation. And they most often did so by finding again how their energy should feel.

MOLLY BARKER

AND THE FACT IS WE ARE WORTHWHILE
JUST BY BEING BORN. I DON'T HAVE TO DO
ANYTHING TO BE WORTHWHILE — I JUST
AM. I AM COMPLETE.

LOST

*H*ow should one feel?

There are many obstacles to experiencing flow or resonance, or the zone. These might include lack of energy (lack of passion), lack of innate (genetic) skill, superior competition, and living too much outside-in listening to others' definitions of success (as Jeff Rouse did). Another one is focusing too much on results, something that Jeff learned the hard way. In a results-oriented world this is a common phenomenon. Some if not most believe that results are the only thing.

When professionals begin with this assumption, they naturally begin to focus externally and lose focus internally and stop paying attention to how they feel — despite the fact that when asked all will say that how they feel affects their performance. Paying attention to others, as Jeff did, and believing their assertions can lead to an internal anomie, a sense of being lost. Here's what Jeff said once:

> *"Writers began to tell me, Jeff, you have to win the Gold Medal. World championships don't matter, world records don't matter, only the Gold Medal matters. And through it all, I began to believe them. And I decided that's what I want to do, go to the Olympics and win the Gold Medal."*

So when a person practices and prepares and then tries to do something, as Jeff did in 1992 in Barcelona, and it doesn't work out, it's a major setback, an obstacle, a barrier. The typical reaction is one of two things: either to give up or to say to one's self, "I have to work harder." People give up because they don't love the practice enough, they don't love the thing itself enough, they only *think* they want the success.

People who really love writing write whether they are published or not. People who really love painting paint whether they sell or not. People who love acting act whether they can make a living at it or not. Those who are focused on the reward, on the return, on the results, will give up if they don't get rewarded along the way. Their definition of success is less the doing of the thing and more the accolades that come along with it. But there's a hollowness in this that one may only discover after years of investment. The research literature has long since made the point: token rewards lead to token learning.

I see this in the business leadership realm. There are it seems to me at least two kinds of leaders. Type 1 leaders seek the benefits, the corner offices, the fancy offices, the cars, etc. Type 2 leaders don't care about the perquisites, they focus on something they want to do and something they want to make happen. I think it's the same with all kinds of performance. I meet people often who say, "I want to be a writer" or "I want to be an actor" or "I want to be an investment banker" or some other well-known profession. Yet when you ask what they've written or what they've played in or what deals they've done, they'll say, "Oh, I haven't started yet." And I know they won't make it because writers have been writing from an early age, musicians have been playing from an early age, inventors have been tinkering from an early age, and investment bankers have been pouring over the *Wall Street Journal* from an early age.

The Irony of External Success

External success, oddly, creates another kind of obstacle. If you love a thing, you practice it, and you get good at it, you're likely to perform well. If you "succeed" in the eyes of the world, you might find that success becomes something that keeps you from the flow you feel when you *do* the thing you love to do. If you love golf and play well and win the US Open, you might find yourself spending lots of time on television, doing ad campaigns, and conducting corporate outings — time which you otherwise might have spent competing on the golf course. If you are an excellent surgeon, you might find yourself promoted into administration and spending less and less time in the operating room. If you're Bill Gates, you might find yourself spending more and more time in business management and less and less time developing new products. Note that Gates finally relinquished his daily managerial responsibilities to go back to his first love, innovation. Intuitively he realized what many in Doug's sample have realized — that if success takes away from you the very thing you love, doing the thing, it's an obstacle to feeling the way you want to feel, to being in the zone, to experiencing flow, to being in resonance.

Consider a good friend of mine. At age sixty, he'd accomplished more than most people in the business world. He'd become the CEO of a major division ($59 billion) of a major corporation. He was newly retired, had wealth in the bank, and yet something was missing. He'd had heart bypass surgery, he was in the middle of a divorce, his kids were grown and gone, and ... he said:

> *"I'm not in a good place. I feel empty. Lonely. Alone. Sad. Never been lost. I must figure out what to do: Make some changes!"*[1]

---

[1] Excerpted from "The Life and Career of a Divisional CEO: Bob Johnson at Honeywell Aerospace (A)," UVA-OB-872, page 1.

"Never *been* lost." My friend is not alone. There are thousands of stories like his filling books like *Career Success, Personal Failure,*[2] *The Failure of Success,*[3] *Must Success Cost So Much?*[4] and *The Future of Success.*[5] What seems patently clear to me is that these people yielded to a common pervasive pressure — letting the outside world define for them what it means to be successful and doing that in terms of external results alone. They work hard to achieve the milestones Doug outlined in a previous chapter and then find themselves having ticked off all of the boxes and still not feeling good inside. In essence, what's happened is they've become cut off from their internal life's dream, that is, how they wanted to *feel*.

They may never have been fully aware of this internal dream — even though Doug would argue that we've all felt it sometime or other as children — that feeling of unbridled curiosity, engagement, bottomless energy, and complete commitment to a thing. Yet after years and decades even of working hard to do what they're supposed to do, they wake up one day and say, "Wait a minute, I've done all that and it doesn't feel good."

Consider the man living in Los Angeles who traveled extensively to build his business. His business was growing and becoming more and more profitable. One day, when he was atypically at home, his wife lined up his seven children, all dressed up in their finest suits and dresses, and said, "Let me introduce you to your children." Or the highly respected church official who traveled extensively to inspire others and was known to his own children as "Mr. Church" because of his travels. Moments like these provide opportunities to reconsider one's work-life balance and

---

[2] Abraham and Rhoda Korman, *Career Success, Personal Failure*, Prentice-Hall, 1980.
[3] Alfred Marrow, *The Failure of Success*, Amacom, 1972.
[4] Paul Evans and Fernando Bartolome, *Must Success Cost So Much?* Basic, 1981.
[5] Robert Reich, *The Future of Success*, Knopf, 2000.

the potential consequences of continuing with one's historical decision patterns.

Figure 13.1 shows a diagonal slash that indicates the barrier that many begin to feel in their lives when they stop paying attention to how they feel. Focused on external results, usually financial or fame related, they come to believe that "professionals will do what they have to do regardless of how they feel" and make decisions accordingly. They run into what Doug calls the "Obstacles" barrier, which includes Setbacks, Obstacles and oddly Success. Success can be an obstacle to feeling how you want to feel because it can divert you from doing the thing you like to do. When you "succeed" and go, for example, on the talk show circuit, you are getting fame but are not doing the thing you love to do. This is what eventually caused the Beatles, for example, to stop touring.[6] The tours became more about screaming fans who couldn't hear the music and fighting all of the things that go *around* touring rather than playing music.

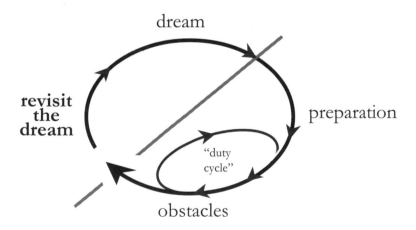

Figure 13.1. Breaking through obstacles by revisiting your internal dream

---

[6] See Pattie Boyd's autobiography, *Wonderful Tonight: George Harrison, Eric Clapton and Me*, Three Rivers Press, 2008.

When people hit obstacles, when they try and fail, most tell themselves they have to work harder and unwittingly put themselves into an obligatory mindset. This bouncing back and forth between obstacles and practice, failure and rehearsal, can become an energy-sucking vortex, a downward whirlpool that can sink a person's efforts to perform at their best.

Whether one loses touch with how one wants to feel from living too much outside-in, from under-preparing compared to the competition, from focusing too much on results — however one loses touch with one's internal dream — when one loses flow, one wants intuitively to re-connect with that feeling. For many, this desire is very weak because they don't believe it's possible. For those in Doug's sample, this desire was strong and came to the fore, intentionally or intuitively. The question is how does one do that, how does one re-connect with the passion (McCammon calls it *magic*)[7] we felt as children.

This is a very practical thing. At first, this approach involves an outside-in intentional intervention in which someone who knows how guides the professional to re-focus on how they want to feel rather than on what they want to do. There's a paradox here, a paradox that bothers many professionals. Yet this focus produces world-class performance.

---

[7]Robert McCammon, *Boy's Life*, Pocket, reprint edition, 2008.

ELBERT HUBBARD

BLESSED IS THAT MAN WHO HAS FOUND
HIS WORK.

FOUND

I had been working with a world-class competitive archer for about six months when he called me to talk about his preparation for the national championships. He was in a position to win Archer of the Year based on his performance and his thoughts about winning (and not winning) were causing him stress. He even said to me, "I am trying to think about the process, but I keep worrying about not winning. I really want to win."

I asked him if he planned on retiring after the national championships and he laughed. "Of course not. I want to shoot for a long time."

That allowed me to point out that this particular championship then was part of a much larger process, part of a career that would not be defined by one event. If he did what we had talked about, to prepare to feel the way he wanted to feel and everything that entailed, he would find what he needed. If he caught himself thinking about winning or worrying about not winning, I told him he just couldn't stop there.

"Do what it takes to win," I told him. Practice for feel. Have a schedule. Get the rest needed. Play.

I also reminded him to view this championship as part of the larger process, one result in a string of many yet to come. I asked him to learn as much as he could, to slow down and pay attention to what was

working for him during the competition, and also to reflect on what was not working. Every shot, everything he did had a result. He needed to learn and compete at the same time.

When he called me right after the championship, he told me he placed fourth. I expected to hear disappointment. Instead, he felt great.

It turns out that in his first few shots, his bow malfunctioned. Part of his equipment was damaged throughout the competition. He told me that in the past, he would have been angry, frustrated, and hard on himself for not taking better care of his equipment. Instead he learned and competed, and he came in fourth. As a result, he also won Archer of the Year.

He also learned how to respond when something important did not work the way he planned. He realized how good he could be even under sub optimal conditions. And, he learned to take better care of his equipment.

Two weeks later he won the world championship. He told me he could not have done that had he not had the experience with the malfunctioning equipment.

His inner result was confidence, trust, belief, better preparation — inner results that became part of his overall process, a process that continued into the world championship.

Results are not always obvious. Overemphasizing the outside-in results often creates conflict with the inside-out results. Very few people win or achieve anything without the inner results developed over time.

Internal Storytellers

The *storyteller* we grow up with is often the compilation of the stories others tell us about success, stories about the world around us, about how people are judging us. These stories are too often outside-in. They rarely are about process or inner results.

If we view results as part of an overall process, however, then it is important to know how to process our results, to learn from them, to grow. When I played little league baseball one boy on my team was a very good player. Our team went undefeated and won the city championship in large part due to this one boy's abilities.

Along with his abilities came the burden of expectations even before he was twelve years old. When he struck out at the plate, he yelled or cried or threw his bat.

He believed that by acting out, he was showing us he cared and that he was as upset as we were that he let us down. In reality, though, he was interrupting his own process and that of the rest of the team. His personal result became our focus. We knew how much he cared, how much it hurt him to fail. What we didn't see is that he could deal with poor results, with failure, with a better process.

The heart surgeon who I have worked with for 15 years is a great example of someone who understands this process, someone whose livelihood depended on doing things right, on saving the lives of others.

We talk often about the fact that a surgeon could do everything right and still have a bad outcome. They need a way to deal with loss that allows them to grow, to learn, and to re-engage.

After seeing this happen, I sat in the office with the surgeon as he dealt with the loss of a patient. From all indications, the team had done everything they could to save a woman who was a grandmother, a woman who collapsed at her daughter's wedding from an aortic dissection. The surgeon grieved over the loss for the family and over his inability to save her. His eyes teared up as he prepared to go talk to her family.

For all of us, doubt, fear and worry are natural reactions. They keep us grounded and humble. Few of us, however would be asked to go perform life-saving surgery on another father, mother, brother or sister a few hours after grieving for someone else's loss. Yet that is exactly what the surgeon faced.

We talked about why he'd become a surgeon. He wanted to help people, to help people when they needed it most. His father was also a heart surgeon and he'd seen how much he'd done for his patients and their families. We talked about the power his patients' stories held for him, how teaching future doctors was his mission. We pulled out the pictures of other grandmothers whose lives he'd saved. As he leafed through the pictures, he remembered the good he'd done. He re-engaged.

In surgery, there is a phrase *Forgive and Remember* which comes from the title of a book written by someone who spent a year observing surgeons. The book outlines a surgeon's responsibilities and the duty each surgeon accepts. Forgive yourself for the outcome, but remember the lessons. Take responsibility.

Too often people forgive themselves for mistakes or poor results, but in doing so, do not grow or learn. Too often, people remember the lesson yet never get past the pain or self-doubt to re-engage. Doing either without the other it seems irresponsible.

We walked down to see the patient he was to operate on that afternoon. Next to the bed was a picture of the patient and his son sitting on motorcycles. The surgeon asked the patient why he wanted to have surgery, why he wanted to live and how he wanted to feel when he was better. His answer was that he wanted to ride his motorcycle with his son. He loved how that felt and he'd brought in the picture to remind him, to inspire him.

In that moment, the surgeon remembered his father, the times they'd spent together. He recalled the times he'd helped his father with emergencies and around the hospital. He remembered the stories of the medical students he taught.

As the patient described riding across the country with his son, the surgeon's confidence returned. He knew what to do. Forgive and remember.

Sometimes talking is enough, listening allows someone to purge. What I learned from the people I interviewed was that having a true process, one they could experience, made a big difference.

A world-class drummer told me a story of performing live at the Grammies in front of his peers and his heroes in the music business. He was nervous as the lights went up and his group was announced. As he set the rhythm for the band, he scanned the audience with soft eyes, without focus, looking over the mass of people in the audience.

He noticed a woman nodding her head to the beat, her eyes fixed right on him, and his eyes focused back. Until then he was feeling good, relaxed, then he noticed the woman was Meryl Streep. He lost his feel, his groove. He took his eyes off from her, looking for someone to help him get it back. His eyes betrayed him, though. He saw Sting, Bob Dylan, Wynton Marsalis and on it went. These were the Grammies after all.

Finally, he found the wife, his band's leader. He locked onto her smile, a smile he knew, a supportive smile, and he found his feel. No one else probably even noticed his distraction and he probably didn't miss a beat, but he felt the audience invading his internal beat, the rhythm he'd practiced a thousand times. For that moment he felt lost. In seconds, he got it back. He'd responded to his own response when it mattered most.

All of these are examples of people losing their way in critical situations. They are also examples of these same people finding the *feel* again. These were all outside obstacles that produced internal obstacles. These performers knew that the way around the external obstacle was to deal first with the internal impediment. They knew that to achieve the results in arenas they'd freely chosen to perform in, they needed a process that included results, but was not defined by the results alone.

Managing Feel in Organizations

BY FEEL

JEFF PFEFFER

BUT I DON'T SEE WHY EVERYONE SEEMS
SO OBSESSED WITH THE RIGHTS OF
SHAREHOLDERS WHO, GIVEN AVERAGE
PORTFOLIO TURNOVER, OFTEN DON'T
OWN COMPANY SHARES FOR EVEN A
YEAR, WHEN WE CAN BE SO CAVALIER
ABOUT THE RIGHTS OF EMPLOYEES WHO
HAVE MUCH MORE PERSONAL CAPITAL
AND ECONOMIC WELL-BEING AT STAKE.
IT ISN'T JUST SHAREHOLDERS WHO
BECOME DISENFRANCHISED BY COMPANY
MANAGEMENT — EMPLOYEES DO TOO. BUT
UNLIKE CAPITAL, EMPLOYEES CAN'T BAIL
OUT QUITE SO FAST. WITH RIGHTS TO
PRIVACY AND PARTICIPATION ERODING,
MANY EMPLOYEES ARE HEADING FOR THE
EXITS. WHEN THAT HAPPENS, EVERYBODY
LOSES.

Bad Suits

*I*n the previous chapter, Doug described what it's like to be "found," that is to "revisit your dream," that is, to remember and re-engage with how you felt when you were at your best. There are people out there, people performing in highly stressful and highly demanding professions who have learned how to manage this process in their lives. For me, that's huge — that there are professionals in many different professions who have learned how to manage their performance upward by paying attention to how they want to feel and organizing their lives to make that happen more often rather than less. I had no idea this could be so until I met Doug and we began what has become now a 15-year series of discussions/collaborations.

As I've traveled around consulting, doing case research, visiting companies here and there all over the globe, I find that the vast majority of companies seem to be operating under the assumption(s) introduced in the earlier chapter on "professionalism." Somehow along the way we inadvertently teach our highly engaged children, students, and employees to suppress their passions and focus on adult results.

I first encountered this concept in Stephen Covey's Organizational Behavior class at BYU in 1971. Steve was already well-known and something of a local phenomenon even though he hadn't yet published his to-be best-selling book, *Seven Habits of Highly Effective People.* I learned a lot from him.

One day he told a story in class that I've never forgotten. The story is powerful for a number of reasons: it teaches a point, it demonstrates the importance of developing a powerful and memorable leadership voice, and it lays down a fundamental invitation to business leaders. He said:

A man went in to buy a suit. The salesman put a suit on him and put him in front of those three-way mirrors and said, "What do you think?" The man said, "Well, it looks good, mostly, but the right shoulder is a bit low." "Hmm," says the salesman. "We could take it off, send it to the alterer, he'd tear the sleeve off, stuff some padding in there, snip snip snip, and then stitch stitch stitch, and redo it, and then send it back to us and that would take several days at least. It would be a lot easier if you'd just raise your right shoulder a little."

"Hmm," the man says, and lifts his right shoulder a little. "That looks better."

"How about the rest of the jacket?"

"Well, it looks a little full in the body."

"Ah, well, we could send it off to the alterer and he'd cut it up, cut it out, and then stitch it back together and then you'd have a 'repaired' suit. It would be a lot easier (for us) if you'd just tuck your left elbow in a little and take that fullness in the body out."

"Hmm," the many says, tucking his elbow in. "That does look better."

"How about the trousers?"

"Ah, the length is good, and I like the way it hangs, but the seat is a little full."

"Well, again, we can send it off, but it would be a lot easier if you'd just reach behind with your right hand, grab some of that fabric and pull a little."

The man did this and observed, "Yes, that looks better. I'll take it!"

"Okay! Would you like me to wrap it up or would you like to wear it?"

"I'll wear it!"

So the man hobbles out of the store and down the street, right shoulder high, left elbow tucked in and right hand stretched behind and holding on to his seat.

Across the street, two women are watching this. (And I can still remember the gleam in Steve's eye, the impatient grin on his face, the bounce in his step as he proceeded.)

*The one woman turned to the other and said, "**Omigosh**, what **happened** to that poor man?"*

*The other says, "Hmm, I don't know …. but wow, look how well his **suit** fits him!"*

His point was that sometimes, maybe often, we design jobs for people that are like ill-fitting suits. We hire young, talented, energetic people and then we begin to "socialize" them into our corporate cultures. You can't wear that to work. You shouldn't talk like that to the boss. You should have been here on time. Stop fidgeting. Don't interrupt the boss when he's talking. No, you can't spend that. Don't leave until you've got these slides cleaned up. Let's spend the next three hours going over the boss's PowerPoint slide presentation, word for word. I know you put a lot into that project, but we've decided we're not going that way. We don't do that …

And at the end of the year, after a year of hobbling around in this ill-fitting suit, we say to them, alright, good job, now next year, we'd like to see you do 15 percent more. So now they have to hobble 15 percent faster.

How many years can a person do that, hobble around in ill-fitting suits before they've become permanently reformed, like a bonsai plant, in the shape of the suit? How many years of repetition of this keep-your-head-down, feelings-to-yourself behavior can one experience before a cynical, jaded attitude settles in perpetually? Before the dominant thought in the morning becomes, naturally, "What do I *have* to do today?"

The problem here is that those who design organizational structures and processes often focus too much on the results, on the outcomes and not on the experience. The residue of Frederick Taylor's turn-of-the-century time-and-motion studies lingers on in the "scientific" desire to design work that is efficient and "organized." The problem with that is that they often design the energy right out of the jobs.

Not All Jobs are Fun

Ah, you say, there are lots of jobs out there that people don't want to do and we can't all have work that we love to do.

Perhaps. The problem with that argument is that there *are* a minority of companies out there who get this. The Pike's Place Fish Market with twelve employees gets it and they have jobs that few people want to do. The former FMC Aberdeen plant (now a subsidiary of BAE Systems) with 100 employees got it. SAS in Cary, North Carolina with about 10,000 employees gets it. Southwest Airlines with about 33,000 employees gets it. To quote John, the former owner of Pike's Place Fish Market, "You have to have fun at work."

Most executives don't believe that. They don't talk about it. And they don't design their organizations to make that happen. They focus on results in a results-oriented world. Ironically, when they do so, they actually undermine the energy that *produces* results. Two of the brightest lights in the field of leadership and management, Noel Tichy and Warren Bennis are quoted a November issue of *Business Week* as saying:

> "There's no denying that judgment is too complex a phenomenon, too dependent on luck and the vicissitudes of history, too influenced

by personal style to pin down once and for all. What can be said for sure is that judgment is the core, the nucleus of leadership. And that in decision-making, the only thing that counts is winning or losing. The results matter — nothing else."[1]

The problem is that jobs and organizations designed to make shareholders rich are often ill-fitting suits. Who wants to work their tails off so the boss can get rich? Who wants to work their tails off so some unknown faceless shareholder gets rich? They don't. People work passionately for a sense of pride, for accomplishment, for frankly, the feel they get when they work. Far too many executives are designing work and work processes that systematically drain energy out of their people. So what they get is the lower levels on the Buy-In scale introduced earlier.

Have you seen the "polar bear" on the Internet pushing himself into work on Monday morning? Or the "penguin" bouncing and bouncing on his way home from work on Friday? Awareness of these ill-fitting suits has become so common it's become a part of our pop culture. How often do *you* feel like a sleepy polar bear pushing yourself into work?

About these jobs that people don't want. Fish mongering has to be one of those. It's stinky, smelly, requires 14- to 15-hour days in a very competitive, commoditized market. Wages are low. Education levels are low. The work is hard labor. Yet, at Pike's Place for example, they've made a way to change that.

This problem occurs not only in low-tech, relatively uncomplicated jobs and organizations. Take for example the high-tech, highly sophisticated world of heart surgery. When Doug was first hired as a performance counselor for heart surgeons, the residents in the thoracic surgery department rated their educational experience 23rd out of 23 departments.

---

[1]Reprinted from *Judgment: How Winning Leaders Make Great Calls*, by Noel M. Tichy and Warren G. Bennis, Business Week, November 19, 2007, In Depth 072.

Within three years, Doug and the visionary who hired him had raised the resident rating to second. That's a remarkable improvement. It points out that paying attention to *feel* is not just an individual thing. Managing feel can also be an organizational thing.

ROBERT McKEE, *STORY*

"STORY IS NOT ONLY OUR MOST PROLIFIC ART FORM BUT RIVALS ALL ACTIVITIES — WORK, PLAY, EATING, EXERCISE — FOR OUR WAKING HOURS. WE TELL AND TAKE IN STORIES AS MUCH AS WE SLEEP — AND EVEN THEN WHEN WE DREAM. WHY? WHY IS SO MUCH OF OUR LIFE SPENT INSIDE STORIES? BECAUSE AS CRITIC KENNETH BURKE TELLS US, STORIES ARE EQUIPMENT FOR LIVING.

First, Day

First Day

I will never forget the first day I went to talk with the third-year medical students of the Department of Surgery at the University of Virginia's Medical School. They were mad. They didn't like long hours, lots of work, sick patients — and, I suspect, a sense of being overwhelmed.

I had just been hired to help run the clerkship experience, the first apprentice-type part of a medical student's surgical rotation. My only experience with surgery was from my own long list of injuries as an athlete. I could go in and try to apply performance principles to their work or I could simply listen.

After feeling completely over my head and out of my element, I decided to listen to them in the same way I listened to the great performers I had been interviewing for several years. I began asking some basic questions. Why were they here? Why did they want to be doctors? Why was this threatening to them? The conversation and the energy changed.

They all had stories, inspiring, fascinating stories about life and families and their motivations for wanting to be doctors. This was the source of their energy, it was the basis of their dream. To help them, I realized I needed to understand how our system was misinforming that energy — or worse yet, killing it.

We agreed there were about ten obstacles to their dreams of taking care of patients. I went to the chairman of the department and asked him simple questions. Specifically, why did we do some of the things we did? In some cases, they were simply the way things had always been done. No one had ever questioned them before. That took care of about eight of these obstacles. He listened to my argument and agreed.

I went back to the students a day later and told them they would have to live with the other obstacles, but I had eliminated many of the others. I also promised to be their advocate in the process. I requested they take responsibility as well for how they felt each day and not simply hunker down and work.

One of the main changes we made was to acknowledge that only a few of these students wanted to go into surgery as their specialty. So why do all the students rotate for twelve weeks through surgery? We wanted them to know everything every doctor needs to know about surgery. This sounds trivial, but it was far from that. At its core, what we did was to connect their desire to be doctors to what they needed to learn from us during those twelve weeks. It gave the surgery program meaning in their dream. It informed their energy.

When we started, the surgery clerkship was considered one of, if not the worst educational experience for the students. Within five years, we won the award as the best clerkship in the medical school. The dean called me in once to ask how we had done that.

I told him, "We helped them take responsibility for how they feel. We focused more on their learning and less on teaching. We treated them like adults. Curt Tribble, a thoracic surgeon led the way. He was interested in each and every student, resident, and patient. He cares about their story."

Together we added something medical school seems too often to take for granted. Taking care of people is a calling, an intermix of people's lives and stories. We simply enabled the students' stories to have meaning in the system.

Several years into this process I spoke at the National Defense University, the joint institute for military education. I was asked to speak as part of training for military chief information officers stationed all over the world.

At orientation I heard the CIO of the Navy speak. His talk reinforced that feel matters. He talked about feel in terms of stories and the need for people to connect. He reminded us that, "All great leaders have a great story."

I later interviewed him and he spent several hours telling me *his* story of the last several years. I interviewed him soon after the war in Iraq began, after the 9/11 attack. He was honored to have the critical role he and his team were playing, supporting the troops.

As I sat with him, I felt his story, his belief in what he was doing and how he was doing it. Maybe he was the ultimate messenger of what I heard from the others I interviewed. Informed energy. He could have told me about all of his accomplishments which were astounding. But what he shared was his energy, his passion about bringing together the people who formed the network that made this country work. Over and over, he talked about the people he worked with developing the networks that transcended organizations and agencies that brought people all over the world together. He talked about enterprise even showing me a picture of the USS Enterprise from Star Trek, a metaphor for going where no one has gone before.

Then he paused, looked down and talked about overcoming tragedy, about choosing between wallowing when things go bad or waking up to make things work. He told me about the daughter he needed to live for. I sat silently as he paused yet again.

He said to me that we need to *feel*, that feel is our barometer, but that when tragedy strikes we need to make a conscious decision to feel. I did not need to know the details to understand what he was telling me. Feel mattered even when it hurts.

Throughout the interview he spoke in terms of feel, of understanding how others felt, and how to inspire people to bring their best each day. In another interview he did I found similar words that sum up what he was all about, why he believed stories matter, why how we feel matters.

> *"If you are contributing the talents that you possess, in a way that makes you happy, then you will be successful. Follow your dreams. You'll spend a lot of time at work. If your career aligns with your gifts and your passion, then every hour you spend working will be both fulfilling and energizing."*

He felt comfortable telling me this story because he worked in an environment where people felt comfortable telling their stories, where they polished their stories, where they paid attention to how they felt and how together they could work toward their dream.

World-class organizations create a place where stories can overlap and serve each other. They do not motivate people as much as they inspire them. That inspiration comes not from loud speeches or signs on the wall, but from the details, from the day-to-day experiences, by holding people accountable to their role in the organization's mission in a way that reminds people of their own dreams and aspirations.

One of the best books I've read about stories and their uses is called *Story* by Robert McKee, a premier writing teacher in Hollywood. One line in particular stands out. He said, "Story is first and last the experience of aesthetic emotion — the simultaneous experience of thought and emotion."

The best stories, the most useful stories, combine, thought, feel, and feelings in my words. And when these happen simultaneously, world-class performance is expressed if the talent is well developed.

The best stories inform our energy to do meaningful movement, to do work. The best stories inspire and educate our dreams into the actions that make them come true. The CIO also told me something critically important about stories. He said:

> *"You need to know your story, to be able to share it to inspire others. But you also have to know the story and to be able share it because we are all confronted with the counter-story over and over. Why we will fail, why things won't work. The better you know and live your story as well as your organization's story the easier it is to keep it alive."*

In all of the interviews I've conducted over the years, the people came alive, leaned forward looking me right in the eye as they felt what they liked best about themselves, about their stories. Their hands danced as they told me in great detail about doing their work, *powered by feel.*

Some of those I interviewed came most alive talking about their companies, their teams, their organizations. Musicians raved about their band-mates. Pilots quietly shared with me the importance of their squadron members and their instructors. Surgeons talked about their mentors, the members of their team, including their patients. CEOs recounted the moments in the "war room" with those trusted few who would tell them the truth. Most of them talked about their families.

That day as I sat and listened to the CIO of the Navy tell me his story, tell me about the importance of story to anyone aspiring to lead, I remembered what Robert McKee wrote, that a good story was not enough. "Your goal must be a good story well told."

McKee described what the CIO, what all of the people I talked to, were telling me about their teams:

> *"Good story means something worth telling that the world wants to hear. Your goal must be a good story well told ... It is the concert of techniques by which we create a conspiracy of interest between ourselves and the audience. Craft is the sum total of all means used to draw the audience into deep involvement, and ultimately to reward it with a moving and rewarding experience."*

KENNY CHESNEY

MY VIEW IS THROUGH A TOUR BUS WINDOW; HIS [IVAN'S] VIEW IS OF THE TIDE COMING IN AND GOING OUT. THERE'S AN UNSEEN MAGIC IN THOSE PLACES THAT CAN BE LIFE-CHANGING, AND I'M LIVING PROOF OF IT. YOU CAN LOSE YOURSELF AND FIND YOURSELF AND REINVENT YOURSELF.

Identity

IDENTITY

*T*elling your story.

What does one say? What's socially acceptable? The best parts only? The worst parts only? Nothing because *they* shouldn't know? They don't *need* to know? Who *are* they to know? My story, after all, is me. It's who I am. Dare I share that with others? What if they reject who I really am? Familiarity breeds contempt after all.

Noel Tichy at the University of Michigan introduced a way of using the principle of telling your story in management in his book, *The Leadership Engine*. He encouraged leaders to clarify their life's stories so they could improve their influence with others. Over the years, I've adapted that exercise.[1]

A conversation with Doug actually inspired that adaptation. Doug loves music. I grew up being taught and thinking that most popular music was evil. I often heard that over the pulpit. Plus I couldn't do much, couldn't concentrate, when I was listening to music, so I didn't listen to it much, except in the car or in church.

One day, Doug said I should read this book by Jimmy Buffett.

---

[1] My adaptation, Life's Story Exercise, is available through the Darden School Business Publishing, online at www.CareerNextStep.com and in my book, *Level Three Leadership*.

Jimmy Buffett? Wasn't he the guy who modeled alcohol, drugs, hedonism, women, sex, and beach parties? Why would I want to read that?

It turns out that Jimmy Buffett wrote his life's story in 400 words or less as a preface to his book, *A Pirate Looks at Fifty*. I read Buffett's preface — and the whole book. It was remarkable.

From my study and teaching of careers classes for 30 years I knew about self assessment tools and techniques. I knew that what people put in and what they left out revealed much about who they were and how they thought.

I'd concluded over the years that when people talk about "personality" or "identity" what they were most often referring to, often unknowingly, was the collection of VABEs (Values, Assumptions, Beliefs, and Expectations) that each person had accumulated over the years. What did they deep down, often semi-consciously, believe about themselves?

Only 400 words. It's a great discipline. First, the page is blank. It's the ultimate projective test, more so than the famous Rorshach Inkblot Test which has stimuli on the page. You can only write on that blank page what's inside you. You can't cheat on a blank page. Only 400 words. With that limit, you can only put in the important stuff. The highlights. The major ups, the major downs. What would you write? Try it. Only two rules: it's *your* life story. And only 400 words. Here's mine:

> *I was born James Gordon Schlafke into a converted chicken coop in a tiny mountain mining town in Idaho. Mom said she used to overfeed me to quieten my fussing. My first memory is being left with the babysitter. By age eight, I'd learned to drive, hunt, and harvest hay. We moved to Boise. I was a latch key kid and played baseball. Dad was a successful contractor but an abusive alcoholic. Mom was a bulimic dental assistant. I learned to fear recognition and judgment. My parents hated each other and divorced when I was 12. They negotiated a deal which allowed her to change my name if he didn't have to pay child support. I became James Gordon throughout high*

school. Mom remarried and we became zealous Mormons. I needed a passport to serve a mission. My stepdad adopted me, and I became James Gordon Clawson. My stepdad was kind, but Mom did all the parenting. I tried to be perfect. I lived in Hong Kong and Japan. I graduated with great distinction from Stanford and couldn't do anything. I went to BYU six weeks late and got an MBA. I became a banker, was bored, aging, and unmarried. At thirty I was smart, clueless, and a virgin. I went to Harvard to get a doctorate, got engaged, broke up, and married the daughter of a pharmacist after dating two weeks. HBS and Susan taught me a lot. A colleague committed suicide over promotion, and we moved to Virginia. Darden offered variety, and I loved it. We had four children each with problems. My Mom moved in next door. I became a church leader. I learned a lot but it nearly killed me. I started over; stepped away from religion. No one really knew me. I found some men with whom I could, for the first time ever, talk about anything. One died; I tattooed his initials on my wrist. Doug taught me about feel. Susan became the most unconditionally loving person I've ever read about or met. I traveled the world and tried to make up for lost time. I ruptured both quad tendons, got sued, and my son presented paranoid schizophrenia. At 60, I feel both fortunate to have done more than I dreamed and sad that life's so short. There's so much more I want to learn and experience. (395)

Here (Figure 17.1) is what my experiencing of that "life" felt like to me emotionally.

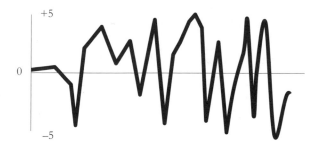

Figure 17.1. Jim's life story chart of emotions

The emotional side doesn't appear much in the story I wrote, but it's represented here. Everyone can do this, that is, write their story and chart their emotions. It's the next, analytic step that I find powerful and impactful. There are at least two ways of using this information. One would be to analyze the Life Story looking for the habits, the themes that keep recurring. In Jimmy Buffett's version two obvious themes or habits that jump out are "tends to break things" and "loves music." In mine, one might see "loves to learn," but "learns too late," and "values honesty and truth." There are more themes in both examples; these are just illustrative.

The second method would be to pick out the highs and lows as indicated on the emotional chart and then reflect and identify the lesson that one took from each event. These "lessons in life" are indeed where our VABEs come from and what make up, literally, our personalities (brain chemistry assumed to be equal, which it's not). Some of the lessons I learned were "marriage is bad," "you can't always believe what you're told," "not being known is lonely," "when in doubt work harder," and "how you feel is much more important than most people think." Here's (Figure 17.2) a partial example of what mine might look like.

Event	Lesson Taken Away
Dad was alcoholic	Stay on the walls, avoid being seen.
Parents Divorce	Marriage is dangerous; avoid it.
Went to Stanford, Harvard	Loves learning, status
Did what Mother, Father, Church told me to do	Living too much outside-in is dangerous: eventually you pop.
Never talked with anyone about everything until 48	Living unknown is lonely
Overfeeding as a child	When in doubt or stressed, eat.
Doing what I was told	Work before play, work is never done.

Figure 17.2. VABEs emerge from lessons in life

Along with the pivotal events in a person's life there are the daily little repetitive things that one hears and/or experiences early on. One way I found out about my early conditioning was to ask my Mom one holiday, "What were you trying to teach me when I was little? You write that down and I'll write down what I thought you were teaching or what I took away, and then we'll get together and compare notes!" We did this. It was fascinating.

Early in life I was taught, among other things, to believe that who you are is what you do. Straight As means you're a good student. This was not a verbal message, but a behavioral one. It was contained in the reactions to grades, to doing or not doing homework at night. Doing your chores means you're a responsible person. This resulted in an achievement orientation to life — and in fact, it served me well in many ways. It got me to Student of the Year in high school, graduating magna from Stanford, and getting a doctorate at Harvard. In the end, though, it was not sustaining. At 48, I had to start over or die. The drive to achieve, to constantly Be Better (which I once put on my license plate), was literally killing me. Achievements, goals, and "to-do"s I've learned are on the outside. And beneath them is again that debilitating assumption: PWD WTHTD **ROHTF**.

It's hugely ironic to me that I spent 35 years of my life organizing all that I did around the concept of "inspiration" and yet felt so clueless after half a century of living. "If God spoke to ancient prophets, and if he were unchanging and eternal, why wouldn't he speak to modern prophets?" That argument made eminent sense to me at 14. "And you, too, can be inspired from on high" was also inspiring. The observations I made over the years, though, suggested some concerns: inspiration seemed capricious, you never knew when it would come or not, and reasonable others claimed equally fervently but with different conclusions that *they* had been inspired from on high as well.

Inspiring means putting energy in. Over the decades, I've come to believe that leadership is about managing energy, first in one's self and *then* in those around.[2] Have you figured out how to put energy and inspiration in your daily living?

---

[2] *Level Three Leadership* begins with that sentence.

B R E N D A   U E L A N D

I learned from them that inspiration does not come like a bolt, nor is it kinetic energetic striving, but it comes to us slowly and all the time. I learned that you should feel not like Lord Byron on the mountain top, but like a child stringing beads in kindergarten — happy, absorbed, and quietly putting on one bead after another.

Inspiration

INSPIRATION

I started using the Jimmy Buffet exercise with groups by accident. I loved the idea of describing one's life in 400 words or less so I sent the Buffet story to my friends to hear their thoughts. Their reactions were fascinating. They would either judge Buffet or they would describe him as "happy" or "sad" although he used few if any emotional words in the description. It is simply a statement of some facts in his life, limited to 400 words.

Those who judged him as good or bad, carefree or lazy or irresponsible were giving me insight into themselves, not necessarily insight into Buffet. I knew that because I'd followed Buffet for years. I even knew people who were his friends. He seemed to me to be none of the characteristics people thrust upon him. He is a self-described workaholic who is one of the most prolific and successful musicians and businessmen you'd come across.

It seemed that people felt compelled to inject emotion into their descriptions, although he gives little or no hint in the description of his emotional life.

I started using this in my workshops to see if the pattern held — and it did. It seemed to be a mirror of the reader's life far more than it was Buffet's story.

We feel and think stories. We feel and think our lives. How we feel is not limited to understanding our emotions either. Feel has to do with how we care for ourselves — eating, sleeping, exercising, and so on. Inspiration makes us want to take care of ourselves. When we do not do these things wisely, all we are left with is emotion. We abandon our own story.

Why does that matter? The less someone knows about us, the more likely they will fill in the blanks. It is human nature. Our minds are designed to predict, to prepare for the emergency that might happen in the next few seconds, minutes or hours. When it comes to blank space, to something unknown, we try to fit something new into familiar patterns. At times, we fill the blank space with our own feelings or memories of similar situations. We place fear where hope belongs, judgment where caring might help, and it places a wall where a door is needed.

World-class performers take responsibility for their own story because it allows them to make good decisions about their future. They choose organizations that match their stories. There is a good fit between the energy and information of the people and the organization. And just as they would not define themselves by a brief description of their lives, they would not choose to work for organizations defined only by a bottom line or annual report. Those are part of the story, but not the most important part.

When I walked into that room of medical students, I needed to know what informed their energy. I needed to know their stories. I was able to adapt our educational process to the overlap of the stories. For those who struggled to find an overlap, I met with them one on one.

Why are stories so important to this process? What do they have to do with what I learned about inspiration from the people I interviewed?

Consider this. Curt Tribble received a letter from one of his former college professors. He had visited us at the University of Virginia and he listened to the philosophy we employ to educate the students and residents. In the letter, he included a section of a speech his brother had given recently. I'll never forget the first time Curt showed it to me. We were preparing for orientation of the students. Curt pulled out the letter and said he wanted to read it to the students, but didn't think he could make it through it. It was too emotional. I took the letter from Curt and said I would read it to the students. I read through it, handed it back to Curt and said, "You're on your own." Curt made it through fine, his low tone of voice making it that much more dramatic for the students.

> *"In the course of trying to persuade my father to go to Italy with me, I gave him a book. The book was titled 'The Architecture of the Italian Renaissance' by Peter Murray. In the introduction to the book, the author eloquently describes the sources of Renaissance architecture and makes the connections to the history and philosophy and religion of the times.*
>
> *My father was never an avid reader, but one day about seven years ago, I sat with my father in his living room. As I was reading the newspaper, my father sat down in his rocking chair beside me and began to read. After several minutes I looked up and was greatly surprised to see there were tears in his eyes, tears rolling down his cheeks. I said, 'Dad what's wrong?' He looked up at me and in a voice almost anguished, he said to me: 'Why didn't I ever know these things? Why did I never learn this?'*
>
> *He went on to explain that, at Georgia Tech, where he had gone to school to learn to become an architect, all they had ever taught him was how to design a building, how to build a building. They had never encouraged him to look beyond this, to explore the whys and wherefores of the architecture, to probe beneath the surface of technique or to make those vital connections between architecture and religion and philosophy and history. Just how to build and nothing more. And in that moment, there was such a sense of loss, of profound sadness at my father's realization of what had been missing all those years laboring in his profession, sweating to meet deadline after deadline after deadline."*

A story. The room was silent for several moments. The students understood. If there is no story, no feel, no overlap, there is no *why* informing our energy, only a *how*. And if the why is born out of fear, it shuts down our energy. Because fear is often the result of living out someone else's story, not your own, when we hit an obstacle, we look to others to tell us how to respond and we give away our natural freedom.

Inspiration happens in the overlap of the why and how, in the fitting together of our stories and our organizations' stories. Great companies have great stories to tell, the stories of their people doing work together, more powerful, than if they stood alone. Great companies offer a place for great stories to happen, a place for great stories to come true.

The medical students at the University of Virginia had amazing stories. A refugee had escaped from Iran spending weeks hiking with his family across the mountains. A grandson watched his grandfather die from a heart attack right in front of him. A woman breathed life back into a drowned swimmer now pursued her degree in emergency medicine. A country kid from Southwest Virginia, the first in his family to graduate high school and go to college returned to care for his community. A woman whose father died of cancer when she was a child went on to study oncology.

The people I interviewed who ran companies, led organizations, captained teams defined inspiration as the power of such stories woven together into a single force that keeps them alive, that makes of them for them a living place.

D A V I D   G R A Y ,   *M U S I C I A N*

I still feel like I am at the beginning.
I'm always learning. I think that is a
sign that you are on the right path.
It's not something you gain mastery
over You are always playing second
fiddle to it. Where does it come from,
the force of songwriting, the drive
to want to do more, to get closer to
the Holy Grail. It's relentless. I find
that sometimes you write songs and
they just come out of nowhere and
it doesn't happen that often, but all
I know is that the more songs you
write and the more time you spend
writing, the more often it happens.

Learning

LEARNING

*M*aking life a "living" place.

It seems to me that most of us, deep down, want to do that, yet many if not most of us end up in jobs and organizations that squeeze the probabilities of interesting living out of us. This squeezing I guess begins with parents teaching us what's okay and what's not okay. We learn that quickly. Then, when we go to school, the okay/not-okay lessons continue the range of acceptable behaviors narrows like the chutes leading to the branding station on a cattle ranch. At the branding station, graduation, society puts its mark on us and we are pronounced a bachelor of science or a master of business administration or a doctor of medicine. We are branded "learned."

Oops. Beware. Eric Hoffer once wrote, "In a world of change, learners will inherit the earth while the learned shall find themselves perfectly suited for a world that no longer exists." (*Ordeal of Change*)

Beneath my "story" there is an intense desire to know the way things are, the way things work. Much of what I'd learned over time, ironically, became an obstacle to continued learning. When news of Peter Senge's work at MIT came to us at Harvard, I remember thinking, that's weird, organizations can't learn, only people learn. Several years later, after learning more and realizing I knew less and less, I acquired a copy of his new book, *The Fifth Discipline*.

To my surprise, I couldn't put it down and read it word for word front to back. His message, that learning how to learn was critical for both individuals and organizations, echoed the assertions of Chris Argyris at the Harvard Ed School. I'd thought myself a pretty good learner over the years — but I began to realize that I'd learned only what others had told me was important to learn. Somewhere along the line, I'd "learned" that "they know best." That unexamined mental habit became a kind of intellectual cage for me.

"How do people learn?" is a tough question. There are books and books on the topic, some distinguishing between child and adult learning. Many factors seem to be critical. Genetic endowment is important. Imitation is important. Variety in context is important. Brain chemistry is important. The expectations of big, powerful others (BPOs or "adults") is important. Channel and methodology are important.

David Kolb asserted that we learn through a four-step process that begins within a few days of birth. First, something happens. We have a concrete experience (CE). Something hurts. Something feels good. Something falls. Something appears. Something disappears.

Then, at some point, we begin to be able to reflect on what happened. This reflection observation (RO) is necessary in order to make some sense of the event. I dropped my pacifier and my Mother came running. I cried and Mother came running — or didn't.

As our neural-neural nets continue to expand, we begin to form memories of historical events. How this happens is still a mystery, but what a fascinating one. As we reflect more and more on events and their meaning, we begin to draw connections. *When* I dropped my pacifier, Mother came running. One way to get attention is to create helplessness or dependency.

This process of sense making Kolb called Abstract Conceptualization (AC).

Abstract conceptualizations form our world view, what we think about how things work, what later will become both Level Two conscious thoughts and Level Three semi-conscious VABEs about the way the world is or should be.

After we've constructed, however rudimentarily a small but expanding world view, we begin to try things out. I wonder (vaguely) if I threw my pacifier down if my Mother would come running? So, we try it, and sometimes our fledgling hypotheses work and sometimes they don't. And the result of that experiment — Active Experimentation (AE) is Kolb's fourth step — becomes another concrete experience. Kolb's model looks something like Figure 19.1:

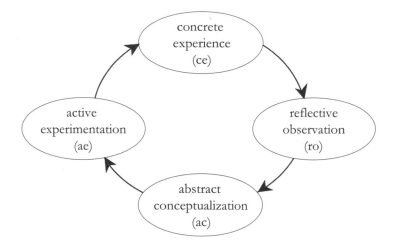

Figure 19.1. Kolb's learning cycle

Kolb asserted that we went through this learning cycle dozens and dozens of times a day, in fact, every time something happened in our lives. Notice that the four steps represent opposites on two dimensions, abstraction and action. CE and AC are opposites on the abstraction scale, and AE and RO are opposites on the action scale. Kolb argued that as we go around this cycle, moment by moment, we develop characteristic patterns or habits in the way we linger on one step or another and not on the others.

These patterns could be as shown in Figure 19.2.

In this example, the individual has developed, over time, a tendency to linger more on reflection and conceptualization and less on action, perhaps more like an academic than a practicing manager. Kolb also suggested that we might affix a single point to a person's learning style by finding the differences between AC-CE and AE-RO and then plotting that point on the four quadrants shown in Figure 19.2. He named the four quadrants to put a label on those whose calculated scores fell in one quadrant or another.

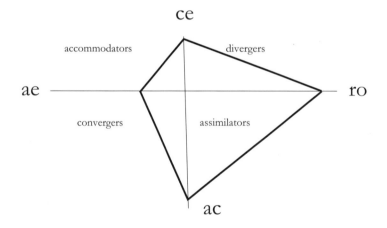

scores computed by ae-ro and ac-ce

Figure 19.2. Kolb's learning styles

This is primarily a cognitive model, that is, it focuses on what people think more than on what they feel or do. Kolb would assert that the feeling part comes along with the concrete experience and the doing with the active experimentation. Yet most of the model tends to focus on cognitive learning.

This brings us back to the question of the relationship between thoughts, feelings, action, brain chemistry, electrical impulses, genetics, instincts, and hormones. How we learn is, it would seem, a complex combination of all of these elements interplaying with the others.

Where is the role of *feel* in learning? Society sends a massive volume of messages to young children when they go to school that *feel* is going to be a lot less important in life than it used to be. Elementary school children are told to begin behaving the way they are "supposed" to and to develop new habits about how one learns.

For many that cycle becomes Read → Listen → Study → Memorize → Regurgitate → Forget. So what they learn in the process, ironically, is that learning is not fun. I see this a lot even among our 30 year old graduate students.

In the end, though, learning seems to me an individual challenge. I go back to Csikszentmihalyi's question: will you ever be anything more than a vessel transmitting the VABEs/memes and genes of previous generations on to the next? In fact, learning can be its own obstacle as Hoffer suggested above.

Levels of Analysis for Learning
Global
Societal
Organizational
Work Group
Individual

We can ask Csikszentmihalyi's core question at the global, societal, organizational, work group or individual levels. Adaptation and positive learning are important, I believe, for survival at all those levels. Arie deGeus in *The Living Company* asserted that learning may be the only source of sustainable competitive advantage. I agree.

Yet if humans behave habitually at the 75, 85, and 95 percent levels at Levels 1, 2, and 3, what are the odds that they'll learn what they need to learn before they die? History is replete with story after story of societies who didn't learn fast enough. And of organizations who didn't learn fast enough. And of managers who didn't learn fast enough. My colleague, Alec Horniman, often asks his students to name their top five values in life. When they're done, he'll ask, "Is learning on your list?" Usually it's not, in the vast majority of cases, even when he or we ask that question in a university setting!

My wife reads voraciously. It's one of her favorite ways of dealing with her ADHD; it calms her mind. She goes through book *series* like I go through a single volume. She likes adventure and exploring, so she began reading one day about someone I'd never heard of, Sir Richard Burton.

"The actor?" I say.

"No, dummy, the explorer!"

"Oh. Who was he?"

"Well, he was British, he lived in India, he translated the Karma Sutra (my ears pricked up), and he explored the Far West, the Middle East, Central America and Africa. He learned dozens of languages and cultures and traditions."

So, I read one of his books. What an amazing man. What I found so amazing (at 55) was that he so *early on* developed an ability to learn despite what his culture and background and training and society were all telling him. He let his own curiosity and attention to the real thing, not someone else's perceptions, guide him. He lived inside-out in a major way.

I find that admirable.

How does one learn to live more inside-out? How does one learn to protect that thing inside that is the repository of curiosity and passion and enthusiasm when all the teachers are saying, sit still, memorize this, wake up, stop fidgeting, do your homework, color inside the lines, and no, do it this way!

How does one overcome the principles of control theory[1] that every parent wields over us like machetes? Did you know that there are three assumptions/VABEs that all parents worldwide regardless of culture share? No?

1) I know what's right for you.
2) I have a right to *tell* you what's right for you.
3) I have a right, nee sacred responsibility to *punish* you if you don't do what's right for you.

What parent anywhere does not believe those three things? They are, Glasser says, the core of "control theory."

How does one break out of the chains of control theory — if at all? And particularly how does one do that with some of the additional insight offered here that it's not only what you *know* that counts but perhaps more importantly what you *feel?*

How does understanding the relationship between *feel* and performance affect the way one attempts to *educate*? How do you do that in an organization? Or as a manager? Or as a parent? Or as a coach? Or as a teacher?

---

[1] Glasser, William, *Choice Theory,* Harper Perennial, New York, 1999.

OWEN D. YOUNG, CHAIRMAN
OF GENERAL ELECTRIC 1934

YOU MUST FUSE AT WHITE HEAT THE SEVERAL PARTICLES OF YOUR LEARNING INTO AN ELEMENT SO STRONG THAT NOTHING CAN DESTROY IT WITHOUT DESTROYING YOU. IT IS NOT ENOUGH FOR YOU TO STUDY ECONOMICS IN AN INSULATED COMPARTMENT AND HISTORY AND GOVERNMENT AND THE LANGUAGES AND THE SCIENCES. IT IS NOT ENOUGH TO GATHER THEM AS SEPARATE PARTICLES INTO A POWDER WHICH YOU CARRY OUT WITH YOUR DIPLOMA. THEY MUST BE FUSED AND INTEGRATED.

Educate

EDUCATE

*W*hy do we learn? It seems to me we learn so we can evolve. We can say it is about growth, about change, about competition, but ultimately, we are given the gift of learning so everything can move forward. I am not necessarily talking about Darwin's idea of survival, but I am not excluding it either. Religion requires learning in order to reach a state of grace no matter what the religion. Sports and Surgery and Mathematics and Physics require "seeing the field" as a whole, transcending the individual skills. And sometimes we learn by unlearning because what we've learned before blocks our path.

The problem is that the "why" we learn as kids might miss the mark as we grow up. We can't learn for pleasing our parents or getting good grades forever. We shouldn't learn in order to pass a test or because we have nothing better to do with our time as we get older. And yet without unlearning those whys, we're stuck.

Further, too often people who instruct merely teach technique, techniques they like and use themselves, without giving us the context or reasons why these techniques may not work at times. Their assuredness produces a false sense of security and, confuses ability to use that technique with skill. The techniques themselves don't help us evolve.

If a heart surgeon believes she is skilled because she has a very good technique, I have no fault with that. Her ability to save lives, however,

probably goes beyond a single technique. If she only had one, and only worked to perfect it, she would without a doubt be left behind.

Unfortunately, we rarely blame the technique, choosing instead to judge the person as behind the times. But when confronted with something new, how can we possibly choose something we do not know. Education should be about increasing our options, about transcending technique. Education should allow us to learn how to create the lives we want and to solve our real world problems.

At the Virginia Medical School, Curt Tribble and I aimed for this sort of education with a very simple strategy. We stopped focusing on teaching and focused instead on learning.

One reason we did this was because the medical profession moves so quickly the answers to the patients' needs change at least every five years. The average training of a physician is five to ten years. This means the answers are changing while they are still learning and while they are actually caring for patients. As Tribble often says, "The answers might change, but the questions remain the same." Education is about asking the right questions and learning to find the right answers across our lifetimes.

Another reason we changed our focus was less obvious and missed by many people. Research suggests we learn through association. We tell stories, we use analogies and metaphors, we make connections. Technique rarely has a story. Education means increasing our associations, making meaningful connections, and putting them to use when they matter most.

A surgeon remembers the feel of hiking the Appalachian trail with his younger brothers, sitting by the campfire, tired and relaxed — and he uses this feel to get through a tough operation. A musician playing in Madison Square Garden recalls the feel of playing in Peoria to remind himself to care more about the music and less about the New York City audience. A salesman reminds himself of the first time he walked into his company, the connectedness he feels to his team as he presents to potential customers.

This is where *feel* comes into play. The more we feel something, the more we remember it. We feel stories better than we feel concepts and certainly better than we feel techniques. We can recall feel best through our own stories.

Maya Angelou said, "I've learned that people will forget what you said, people will forget what you did, but people will never forget how you made them feel."

This is the subtlety of feel. Feel is a skill the way taste can be developed to be a skill. It is not that you can repeat the feel, it is that you can feel what is real. Its true value is that you feel what is real and like your favorite food you can seek out what feels real. Just like you might be able to taste a wine and identify the flavors that inform your energy, feel can be used in the same way.

When doing something feels a certain way, it is easy to believe in that thing (or the person who helped you feel that way), and to want to repeat the experience. What I heard in my interviews was that world-class performers learned to feel how they wanted to feel, how they needed to feel to perform at a high level. Many of the people I interviewed excelled in different careers and areas and could use the feel skill in each.

If you say I only feel that way around those people or doing that thing, however, you limit your skill of feel so that when someone is gone or something is lost, you think you will never feel that again. That is the story the CIO of the Navy was telling me — that you need to feel to find what feels real to you.

The lesson of experience is not merely in the power of what happens around us in that experience. What we learn from the experience is how we *feel*. The more experiences we have, the more feel we learn. Too much of the world today is designed to market products and celebrities to us so we believe their power is in how *they* make us feel and not in *our* ability to feel, in the development of the skill to feel.

The people I interviewed found something that felt so compelling that they built their lives around that *feel*. They didn't build their lives around music or business or being a doctor — they built it around how they felt in those roles.

Moving from inspiration to education means learning to increase our skill of feel, not locking into something outside of us as the source of how we feel. Education is learning the value of stories, analogies, metaphors, and association, not learning a single story and committing to it for all time.

The more we learn to feel and develop our skill to feel, the more we make connections with meaning. The more we look to feel, the easier it is to reevaluate our connections as they diminish or better ones reveal themselves.

To truly become educated, we need overlap, interactions, consequences that go beyond technique because they allow us to evolve, to find our place in the world, to fulfill the promise inside of us. Feel is the most powerful way to make these connections: to learn them and put them to use. The white heat Owen Young described cannot be thought. It must be felt.

I believe we are all born with promise. No one knows what that promise is. We all have different skills at different levels. Few of us can say we are evolved enough to have fulfilled that promise. Maybe we never do. Maybe our job is to prepare the next generation to carry on. Our task is to fulfill it as best we can.

As far as I can tell from my research and from my work, *why* we learn sets the stage to *how* we learn. Accepting the why allows us to experiment with the how. It allows us to adjust.

One Grammy award winning musician I interviewed started out simply playing the music others wrote. He felt that to go to the next level, he had to write the music himself. Eventually, he felt he needed to produce his music as well. In each case, his reason for playing music forced him to learn another skill — from playing to writing to producing. At each stage he tried different techniques and measured his success against his own idea of why he was doing these things. He might have been very skilled in one technique, but he was willing to abandon that technique if he saw he was not evolving.

At the age of forty, after several gold records, he believed he needed to teach his left hand to play everything his right hand could play. This is unheard of. He went back to the woodshed (now also a studio on his property) and practiced for hours, starting from the beginning with scales.

Two years later he emerged and gave several concerts. I was at the first one. The left hand playing independent of the right. It blew everyone away. Later I saw him playing in this two handed style in concert with another successful musician. After the other guy played some of his old songs on the piano, my interviewee walked out on stage, took his place at the same piano and started playing. The other guy paused on stage, turned to look at him then asked "Where did that piano come from?" Why? Because the piano he had just stopped playing now sounded like *two* pianos! Sitting in the audience, I was blown away by the difference in the way these two Grammy Award winners sounded … and he wanted to blame the piano!

Why did the performer I interviewed do this? He wanted be a musician, to play music. And why did he want to be a musician? He explained it to me like this, "I've tried to make my music the best forum for total expression of my personality. The whole search has been a search for myself, a search for me for what is unique to me."

As the Chinese proverb says, "Tell me and I will forget, show me and I may remember. Involve me and I will know."

In surgical education we follow the mantra, "See one, do one, teach one." Feel is at the core of these experiences. When we feel and think, we fire neurons. We wire them together in a more memorable manner and in usable, accessible fashion. We give them life. We build them pathways.

The people I interviewed told me learning was not limited to the instruction they received from others. They mentioned great teachers only because they inspired not because of the specifics of their subject matter.

I interviewed many medical residents and students about their career choice beyond just being doctors. How did the best resident choose to become a heart surgeon, a pediatrician, a radiologist? Quite often it came down to them being around someone who modeled the kind of doctor they wanted to be. Many of the best residents chose their career paths based on the people they came into contact with, not simply the specialty or rotation they were on. They learned first who was worth learning from. Then they found ways to be around them, to operate and round with them as often as possible. The wanted to create a feel.

A Grammy-award winning drummer I have known all of my life learned something similar from our high school band director:

> "That teacher helped us find our gift in life. I was not a good student, but man, when I got into the music department, he treated me like I was The Guy. He treated me like I had a bright future ahead of me. Whether I saw it or not, he saw it. And he was no ordinary guy to be saying it. He would walk into class and look up at the percussion section and say, 'I played with James Brown

on stage last night and it was smoking.' He was at the Howard Theater playing with James Brown. It was such a big deal to us. Not only did he instill some good values in us as for as working, but he was doing it. He had me believing I could make a living at music because he had and because he believed I could."

A five-time world champion canoeist saw East German canoe competitors when he was thirteen. He analyzed a special stroke they used, learned it and modified it for himself. He won the world championship the next year at age fourteen.

When I was little my father was in charge of creating a division in the government to eliminate lead in the public housing. A daunting expensive task. He was given workers from other divisions who were deemed unnecessary. Let's just say they were not excited about it. Removing lead from public housing was an uninspiring task. He rented a van, loaded his team in and drove them to see the people most impacted by the lead. He took them to Children's Hospital where they saw the kids with lead poisoning and the mantra quickly became, "For the children" instead of "Let's remove lead paint." They learned something he could never have told them about.

An international Chairman of Goldman Sachs learned about business at fifteen when his father was hospitalized and he was forced to run his father's oil delivery business. He later entered the Air Force where he saw Chuck Yeager and Neil Armstrong rise to the top. While he knew he would not make a career flying, he learned from observing them how to be passionate about what he did and how to do work.

I always ask people I work with to find role models, to make time to watch them, to talk to them, to learn from them. If they do not find the time, I cannot help them learn what they need to know. I can only help with why someone should do this.

Let me be clear about the education phase of this model. It is about learning to use and develop our skill of feel. This means recognizing that we too easily have an experience, too easily learn a technique or story that becomes our own hammer so that we see the world as full of nails. Feelings, stories, and techniques are singular episodes, singular tools. The purpose of education is to learn and develop the skill that allows us to create stories, store feelings as past experiences of feel, and to embrace and let go of techniques. That skill is *feel*.

Education is about learning and must be modeled, valued, inspired. It is what we do when no one is watching so we can do it when people watch and when it matters most.

BILL GEORGE[1]

AS A CEO, YOUR ATTENTION ULTIMATELY
HAS TO BE ON THE LONG RUN — AND
THAT IS, OF NECESSITY, A LONELY RUN. THE
VOICES CLAMORING FOR YOUR ATTENTION
WILL BE MANY. YOUR JOB IS TO FIND YOUR
OWN.

[1] Bill George on why today's CEOs are being swayed by every voice — except their own, in "Why It's Hard to Do What's Right," *Fortune,* Monday, September 15, 2003.

CONTROL WATCHING

*C*an you perform when people are watching? Can you sing outside the shower? What happens to you when people are looking over your shoulder? Do you freeze? Do you tighten up? Do you become more self-conscious?

Oversight is a big deal in business. Management is in fact much about control and making sure that others do what you want them to do. We often use a model adapted from one originally developed by Noel Tichy at Michigan to overview the main activities that virtually all companies must attend to in order to organize their people. Every organization — of any kind and in any place — must decide *at a minimum* who to bring in (selection), what to have them do (work design), how to assess what they did (evaluation), how to reward them (rewards), how to get rid of them (outplacement), and how to help them grow (learning and development).[2] Whether an organization pays attention to each of those elements and to what degree is important, and whether they do or not, those functions *exist* and will have an impact on the organization's outcomes.

So, one of the first ways a group of people can begin to *become* an organization is to pay attention to these fundamental elements. How *much* attention it (they, management) pays becomes a matter of control. How much control would you like to have over who joins you? This is a national issue, by the way, with regard to immigration. How much

---

[2] If you want to learn more about this model, see *Level Three Leadership 4th edition* by James Clawson.

control would we like to have over what people do? How would you assess what they do? Would you want to control rewards and compensation? Would you want to control who leaves your organization and under what circumstances? What about learning? Would you like to control your organization's ability to adapt and evolve?

I often ask seminar participants if it were your company, if your name were hanging over the door, how much control would you want over your employees. Some want to argue for a while about what "control" means. Over what? At what level? Well, that's part of the point. If it's your company, if you're in charge, you decide. No one else can tell you. Consider the scale in Figure 21.1. Where would you want your level of control to be if it were your company?

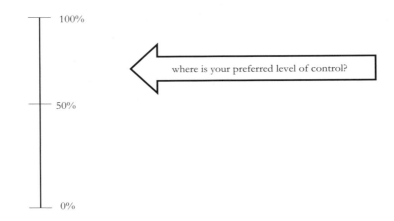

Figure 21.1. Control

One woman in an executive seminar said, "110 percent!"

"What?"

"Yes," she said. "If it were my company, I'd want to know what my employees were doing on Wednesday night, Saturday morning, and

Sunday afternoon. I wouldn't want any of my employees doing anything any time that would reflect negatively on my name or my company."

Wow.

"Zero," another fellow said.

"Really?"

"Yes. Control stifles creativity."

"I note that well, if you had zero control, you wouldn't know if anyone were showing up for work, you wouldn't be getting financial reports, you wouldn't be able to have your thinking influence the company in any way. How could you have an organization with zero control?"

The practical range must be somewhere between the extremes. There are obvious tradeoffs. If you have too much control you stifle creativity and innovation. If you have too little control you lose focus and intent. Where would you put *your* preferred region of control on this scale?

One of the very common ways that managers use to control others is to assess their performance. The judgment of others, performance appraisal, has become a very powerful means of control even if it's not directly tied to compensation and rewards (although the theory goes that it should be, but that's another story). So we'd like to think of work design → assessment → rewards as a nice causal, neatly linked chain, but in reality it often is not.

At the university for example, one's assessment may or may not be related to rewards depending on the budget, the legislature's allocations, and variations in local application of principles laid out by the human resources department. Yet, annual performance reviews create lots of anxiety, anticipation, concerns, and often afterward, anger and resentment.

The whole process of performance assessment can be very debilitating and de-energizing.

How does one manage the process, therefore, successfully? Many organizations spend tons of energy trying to get this right. The literature abounds with discussions about how to do it, how to separate the assessment from the development portions of the process. How to ensure distributive justice and ethical behavior, whether income should be public or not, and on and on and on.

James Goodnight, the co-founder and CEO of SAS Institute in Cary, North Carolina, has noted that no one likes to give performance appraisals, no one likes to receive them, and often they are inaccurate, and they take up enormous amounts of organizational energy from year to year, so he declared, "We just won't do them." Wow!

Some companies have very detailed processes for managing the performance appraisal process complete with schedules, guidelines, criteria, samples, training, consequences for not performing them, and so on. With regard to performance assessment, organizations run the gamut from high levels of control to virtually none.

SAS, by the way, has been extraordinarily successful since its inception. The company has an unusual and powerful business model and clearly, given the above, innovative thinking with regard to how to run/control a business.

At the other individual end of the size scale, Dave Scott has a similar philosophy. Remember his story? We introduced him earlier. When he was 49, he had won six Hawaii Ironman Triathlons.[3] If you're not familiar with triathlons, these are races that include a 2.2-mile swim in the open

---

[3] For more information on Scott's career see http://www.davescottinc.com/. (as of January, 2008)

sea, a 110-mile bicycle ride, and a 26.2-mile footrace back-to-back-to-back.

Oddly, Scott says "During a race, I never wear a wristwatch, and my bike doesn't have a speedometer. They're distractions. All I work on is finding a rhythm that feels strong and sticking to it."[4]

I say, "oddly" because if you consider how most athletes compete it is by time and distance. But Scott avoids mid-race assessment of his results. Instead, he assesses how he *feels*, the rhythm. By doing that, the by-product is that he's blowing his competitors away. He's consciously ignoring how he's doing externally and focusing on how he's doing internally.

What happens to you when someone is looking over your shoulder while you work? What happens to you when *you* become aware of your external performance? Do you "choke?"

I've been in both places. One of my worst professional experiences — no, it *was* the worst — was giving a speech before a large audience to a group I didn't know well. The organization had taken control of my slides and when I got there I realized that I needed to do something else, but I didn't have control of my slides and I knew it wasn't going well and what I needed to do, but I couldn't stop myself or the process. I was aware of my own performance, internal and external, and couldn't change it. I'll tell you more about this experience shortly.

There have been other times when writing, speaking before large groups, or playing sports (basketball and golf) that I was dimly aware of how well things were going both internally and externally and was able to resist that urge to *be* aware — to remain focused on the thing and not

---

[4] Quoted in *Outside* magazine, 9/03, p. 122.

my assessment of it. When I've given in to that, and noted, "Wow, you're doing really great," the next thought is often "don't screw it up."

That has been, for me, usually the beginning of the end.

I once shot a 73, one over par, at the Old Course at St Andrews. At the time it was my career-low round, so very good golf for me. Every shot, save one, went where I aimed it and every picture of what I wanted to do, happened. I had a great caddy, a young patient man named Scotty who gave excellent advice, and I was able to execute. I think it was largely because I was so sick that day, I almost didn't go to the course.

I'd gotten food poisoning the day before and woke up nauseated, diarrhetic, and so weak I could hardly dress. But, it was St. Andrews day. So I went. Scotty said, "Hit it there."

I did without much thinking or worrying. I had no energy for that. Perhaps *that* was the difference.

The US Women's Open in golf was held the last weekend. The world's best players were competing for the highest prize in their sport. My favorite was in the hunt on the last day in the last group. But as commentator Johnny Miller noted, sometimes people want it — the reward — *so* bad, they focus so much on the prize and not on the immediate feel-based process, that they ... "choke" seems like such a strong word; it is perhaps more accurate to say that "their performance declines."

As Doug has pointed out, when one focuses too much on the end result and not enough on the immediate feel, a tipping point is reached, and bad things happen.

There have been times when playing golf or basketball, I've been aware of how well things were going, and feeling good, thought, "Wow, this is going well," and bang! The next five shots in a row bronged off the rim or sliced out of bounds.

Choking? The process is really one of a diverted attention, attention diverted *from* feel and *to* results. Organizations can choke on performance reviews as well. The challenge is to be able to perform on demand.

KATHERINE GRAHAM

TO LOVE WHAT YOU DO AND FEEL THAT
IT MATTERS — HOW COULD ANYTHING BE
MORE FUN?

When It, Ma

WHEN IT MATTERS MOST

*W*e were down three points with six seconds left. We had the ball out of bounds at the far end of the court. My coach, Terry Holland, said, "Dribble down and make the three."

I'd made the shot thousands of times, sometimes literally with my eyes closed, other times while not looking at the basket. I'd made it in summer league games with defenders draped all over me. The night before, I showed an NBA scout how easily I could make the shot.

This time if I missed we would lose the ACC Championship and possibly our number one seeding in the NCAA tournament. National television, 15,000 fans, my parents ... everyone watched.

Here I was when it mattered. This was the thing dreams and commercials are made of. I should mention that I was infamous as a benchwarmer, I rarely played.

Jim Valvano, coach of the opposing team, called his guards together and told them to foul me if I got close to the three-point line. Hearing him say that shook me.

I dribbled down, crossed half court, and they rushed at me... or at least it felt like that. Having watched this on ESPN Classic a hundred times, I had more than enough room to take my shot, the shot I felt confident taking … at least when it did not matter so much. I passed to our point guard, who shot an air ball. We lost.

The truth is I was simply not ready for that moment, a moment most kids (including me) grow up dreaming about. I blew it. I could make every excuse in the world that I was not a regular player, that no one could be expected to be ready for such a moment sitting on the bench all year. I know better now.

How do you do what matters when it matters most?

Now the rubber meets the road. How do we judge that? Who will you allow to judge your performance and maybe by extension you?

It is at this point people get hung up, feel like they've been hung out. Letting someone evaluate your work, inviting criticism is scary, makes us vulnerable. It is also at the evaluation stage you learn the best and the most as long you are willing.

I often talk to medical students about the idea of a social contract. I refer to Thomas Paine's *Common Sense*, one of the most stirring pieces ever written. I do not claim to understand the political science behind the idea of a social contract. However, I find it useful to keep the concept in mind when we do evaluations or assessments of performance and, by extension, of us.

Here is what Paine said about the role of government in the lives of men:

> *"Some writers have so confounded society with government, as to leave little or no distinction between them; whereas they are not only different, but have different origins. Society is produced by our wants, and government by our wickedness; the former promotes our happiness positively by uniting our affections, the latter negatively by restraining our vices. The one encourages intercourse, the other creates distinctions. The first is a patron, the last a punisher.*

Society in every state is a blessing, but government even in its best state is but a necessary evil in its worst state an intolerable one; for when we suffer, or are exposed to the same miseries by a government, which we might expect in a country without government, our calamities is heightened by reflecting that we furnish the means by which we suffer! Government, like dress, is the badge of lost innocence; the palaces of kings are built on the ruins of the bowers of paradise. For were the impulses of conscience clear, uniform, and irresistibly obeyed, man would need no other lawgiver; but that not being the case, he finds it necessary to surrender up a part of his property to furnish means for the protection of the rest; and this he is induced to do by the same prudence which in every other case advises him out of two evils to choose the least. Wherefore, security being the true design and end of government, it unanswerably follows that whatever form thereof appears most likely to ensure it to us, with the least expense and greatest benefit, is preferable to all others."

Society is created by our wants, promotes our happiness, while government is created by our wickedness and exists to restrain our vices.

As I listen to people in their loneliest hours, in the darkest times of struggle, I am reminded how right Paine was.

Defining *government* in our lives is one of the most important things we can do. In a review of the movie *We Were Brothers*, the author finished the article by asking a simple question. "Do we govern or are we governed?" This question is at the heart of the evaluation process for any successful team or organization.

Many people fear the evaluation process because they feel helpless, judged, inadequate. These people feel governed.

World-class performers, however, welcome evaluation. They look forward to it when it is done well, provides useful data, executed by credible people. One swimmer told me about the time he moved from Hawaii to California to train with better swimmers.

> *"When I first arrived, I began training right away. One of the people I trained with was considered one of the best backstrokers in the country. One day we were doing what swimmers call repeats. Basically we were going head to head up and down the pool. He kept beating me, kicking my butt. I wasn't used to this. I was getting mad. He saw that I was becoming discouraged so we stopped and got out of the pool. He grabbed a towel and said, "Hold this towel and as you come through your normal stroke let go of it. Let's see where it lands." I took the towel and did a couple of backward strokes. I let the towel go, and it landed about four feet away from my feet. He picked up the towel and did same thing, but when he let go of the towel, it landed right by his foot. He showed me how to do that. We jumped back in the pool, and I never lost to him again. Several weeks later, I won the National Championship."*

Part of the process is getting good at knowing who to listen to, whose evaluation you invite, and whose evaluation you must accept to get the benefit of whatever compensation you receive. They feel that they govern.

This is the social contract. What do you allow someone else to govern in your life in order to get the benefits of joining an organization so you can govern the rest of your life? What freedoms do you give up? What responsibilities do you accept? What compensation do you expect to get back in exchange?

If you cannot answer these questions, the evaluation process might be accurate in some ways, but it will be incomplete. That lack of completion makes all the difference between governing and being governed. It is this lack of completion I believe that paralyzes us with fear. When that happens, we look to the *government*, in whatever form it takes in our lives, to relieve us of that fear, to make us feel safe. That is precisely what Paine warned Americans about.

The evaluation process is something you do together, not something that is done to you. It is the examination of the overlap between the individual model and the organizational model. It is done, to use Paine's words, to promote happiness and comes from our wants. Too often, however, it is done as a way of restraining our vices.

The simple way to consider the evaluation phase is to ask: Did what you do work? Did you move from where you were to where you agreed you wanted to go or beyond? If so why? If not, why not?

In concrete terms: Did you fulfill your job duties well? Did you meet or exceed the numbers expected of you? Did you finish the projects you took on? Did you succeed based on the agreed upon definition of success?

The tricky part is yet to come, though. How was success defined? What was your role in creating that definition? What is the overlap between your definition and the organization's definition?

Do you govern? Or are you governed?

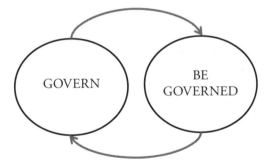

Figure 22.1. Governing and being governed

In my work, I would go back to a person's or organization's inspiration to answer that question. How does your result compare with your dream? Are you and you organization inspired by what you've done and by how you did it? Did the benefits outweigh the cost for you and the organization? Does the evaluation of this process help or hurt your performance, a performance defined by the meaningful movement in the direction of the personal and organizational dream? Does it inspire you and the people around you? If not, it is an obstacle.

Done well, evaluation actually inspires people because it informs their energy. The overlap is a good fit. It allows candid conversations about the work without judgment of the people.

World-class performers constantly check in to see how they're doing. They want to know. They will adjust if need be. They will not be judged by others but they want data about where they are, how they got there, and if they should keep doing what they're doing. They want data, not judgment. Simple.

When I was dribbling up court that night in Atlanta, I was scared. When it mattered most, I simply could not fire. Why? Because I had allowed myself to be governed by fear, by the judgments of others, and with bad data. When it mattered most, I did not know how to govern myself, my own feelings. Too long before I had stopped governing my own life, evaluating my work, and collecting good data. My skills simply weren't there when I needed them.

Instead of taking the shot, I passed off.

PERSONAL APPLICATIONS

FRANK DEFORD, *SPORTS ILLUSTRATED*

SHE SIMPLY LOVES PLAYING. TENNIS IS A JOY TO HER. THAT'S ALL. ... NO, SHE DID NOT NEED TO ALMOST BE KILLED, SHE DID NOT NEED TO LOSE HER GREATNESS TO A MADMAN'S KNIFE, TO BECOME THE FULL, FINE PERSON THAT SHE IS. BUT WE CAN SAY THAT 10 YEARS REMOVED FROM HELL, MONICA SELES HAS WON WITH A GOOD, BRAVE HEART FAR MORE THAN SHE EVER DID WITH A TENNIS RACKET. IN HER OWN SIMPLE WORDS OF PRAISE, SHE'S A HUMAN BEING.

PAYBACK

An international association once asked me to be a plenary speaker after lunch. I didn't know the group well so I was not finalizing my thoughts until the last minute. I'd gone to the conference early to scope out the audience. They were a formal group. There were lots of suits, white shirts, and ties. Very polished, *shiny* shoes. Like Doug, I knew what to do, how to do it, and usually it felt really good. I'd prepared two options, one more academic and one more impactful but a bit of a stretch from the requested title. I'm warming up to the experience looming.

As we readied all of the AV stuff during lunch, to my complete surprise, they took control of my slides in the back of the room.

That one thing, like Coach Valvano's overheard comment, really threw me for a loop. I no longer had control over what I would do at tip off.

The people in the back were in charge.

When it came my turn, with a 1,000 people in the audience, I stood up and … froze.

The people in the back showed my first slide for presentation number one.

I knew that I should do presentation number two, but it was too late. The die was cast.

I was unable to change mid-stream, even though I realized, constantly, continuously, that what I was doing was not what the group wanted or needed.

There was me inside shouting, "Don't **do** this! Do the **other** thing!"

But I couldn't.

It was like being on a large karaoke stage and suddenly they put up a song you don't know. You could hear the groans.

I could feel the pain. It was a disaster.

What's worse, the next speaker was spectacular! She was engaging, poised, and had good content. By comparison, I was a stuffed bear with the mange and nowhere to hide.

My payback came in a different place and time — much later. I was invited again, to my surprise, to be plenary speaker, not to that same group, but to a different group, a group I knew much better.

But still the issue is, "What does one say that will grasp the minds and hearts of a large audience?" In this case, as well, there was a significant intimidation factor. I hadn't been with the group for some time, and the previous plenary speaker the day before was one of the bright luminaries in that field.

Jeez, I'm thinking, how can I follow that?

This time though (and every time since that time mentioned above) I was in control of my slides. I could manage the pace and the topic and give my repertoire on my computer. If I wanted to I could change gears. I could look left, look right, and if all the receivers were covered, I had options.

I did my thing my way. It was more of a conversation really. It felt good to me, and I was enjoying the "relationship in the air" between me and the audience. The sequencing felt right, the words somehow emerged. The timing was good.

When it was over, shock, there was a standing ovation. The president of the organization said she'd never seen that before. I felt that warm afterglow when you realize that you played well, fit the pace of the game, and it was good for all. Not a prideful thing, a realization really that the thing itself, playing the game, was its own reward.

Most of the conversations I hear among MBAs, practicing managers and executives about reward compensation include discussions about how to incentivize people. Everyone wants to know, "What's the incentive? Why should anyone want to do this?" Always the discussion is about pay, recognition, medals, bonuses, time off, raises, perquisites and benefits.

The good folks at Towers Perrin have been tracking executive compensation for some time now. Data stretching over the last almost twenty years have stayed pretty much the same relatively. Consider for example, the ratio between CEO income and the average manufacturing employee's income. Figure 23.1 shows that ratio for several countries. The ratio in

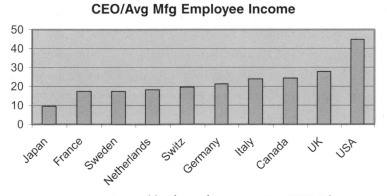

towers perrin, worldwide total remuneration 2003-04

Figure 23.1. Executive pay multiples

the US is nearly twice what it is in most industrialized countries. The difference has grown over the last 15 years.

"Well, that's fine," you say. "The CEO to front line employee income ratio is an indication of the entrepreneurial spirit and of the power of the free market."

Perhaps.

These data also suggest growing gaps between the have's and the have-not's. The problem with that is that eventually as history shows the have-not's rebel and tear the system down. I saw in the news recently that the richest man in India is building a new house for him and his family — a 23-story skyscraper complete with six floors of parking, gyms, pools, theaters, etc. Wow. I wonder how he incentivizes his employees?

The problem with incentives has been aptly described by Alfie Kohn in a wonderful book, *Punished by Rewards*.[1] He says that the problem is that all external incentives to do work systematically *de-motivate* people to work.

That statement is counter-intuitive for most managers.

Consider this simple experiment. If you select people randomly, then randomly divide them into two groups, and ask them to play a board game like *Monopoly*® for two hours explaining that you're going to give them a break after one hour, and then video tape what they do, you find that the group you offered to pay left early for the break, came back late and wanted to leave early.

---

[1] Alfie Kohn, Punished by Rewards: *The Trouble with Gold Stars, Incentive Plans, A's, Praise, and Other Bribes*, Mariner, NY, 1999.

The group that you *didn't* pay, played through the break, and stayed late. These results emerge not just once, but over and over again. It's clear that when you pay people to do a thing, their energy for doing it declines.

Golfer Tom Weiskopf once commented that he remembered exactly the day that he stopped enjoying golf — he said it was the day he turned pro.

Contrast that with a well-known musician Doug described earlier who declares that people pay him a lot of money to stay away from his family, to eat rubber chicken, to stay in lousy hotels, and travel in buses. But, he says, when he goes on stage and the curtain goes up and the camera lights go on, *that* he does for free.

Kohn describes the effect of external rewards in this way:

> *"The more significant problem is precisely that the effects of rewards do last, but these effects are the opposite of what we were hoping to produce. What rewards do, and what they do with devastating effectiveness, is smother people's enthusiasm for activities they might otherwise enjoy."*[2]

The challenge with incentives and external rewards is that people *sense* deep down that if you have to pay me to do this job, it must not be worth doing on its own. We see this in the graduate schools of business. MBAs who want to go to Wall Street and make their fortunes. Some of them love making deals; many of them just want to get rich quick and leave. Most of them leave before they get rich and land back in the alumni career services office looking for help in finding something else. This is another manifestation of the "energy sustainment" problem we talked about earlier.

So how you compensate people is a big deal.

---

[2] Ibid, page 74.

Most of the world focuses on the external measures like money, recognition, title, perquisites, benefits, and company cars or planes.

But is that why people really work? To pay the bills? Surely. That's good enough for large numbers of people. But working for money is a formula for mediocrity. If you want to consider world-class performance, though, you'll have to look deeper.

How would you plan to compensate someone if you wanted them to compete at the world class level?

CHARLES SCHULZ

 I JUST HAVE TO DRAW FROM MONDAY TO
TUESDAY TO WEDNESDAY TO THURSDAY
AND IT GOES ON AND ON AND ON. PEOPLE
SAY "WHY CAN'T YOU WORK REAL HARD,
GET WAY AHEAD AND THEN YOU COULD
TAKE A MONTH OFF." THAT'S FOOLISH. MINE
IS NOT THE KIND OF A JOB I'VE WORKED
ALL MY LIFE SO THAT I DON'T HAVE TO DO
IT.

WORK

*D*espite its title, this chapter is about compensation. It is where all the pieces come together — the individual, organizational, and the overlap. It is also about work and I mean that in the most exciting manner.

Work can be described simply as meaningful movement, from where you are to where you'd like to be. Power is the benefit/cost ratio of the work you do.

Wellth (a clever term I've used for over a decade) is the result of your work and is the sum of meaningful movement and growth in your ability to do work.

This has everything to do with compensation. You could even say these ideas define compensation.

What I learned from world-class performers was that they defined their own form of pay, and it was, believe it or not, all related to their ability to do work powerfully in the direction of *well*th.

They wanted to move from where they were to where they wanted to go in their lives as powerfully as possible and in a way that increased their ability to move powerfully with meaning.

The clearest example I can give you goes back to the Grammy award-winning musician. He loved playing and making music. Therefore, he decided the best way to do that as often as possible was to get good enough as a musician to make a living at it. He also knew that to be a great musician might mean working with other artists for free or doing gigs for less money or working more days than he might want to.

In each case, the form of compensation might be different. One time it might be money, another time meeting new people, learning or increasing his skills in front of an audience. These all helped him move and grow in the direction he wanted life to take him. His compensation is not simply an exchange or payment. His compensation is actually the doing of work in his own life. As he does this work, he can measure it in terms of *well*th (see Figure 24.1) — the skills he acquires and improves, financial fitness, and health, the things he needs to do the work of his life powerfully.

This goes for organizations, too. If you look at a company you might invest in, you want to know not just that it increases its wealth, but that in doing so it is increasing its ability to grow, to sustain a certain level of performance so it can compete in the future.

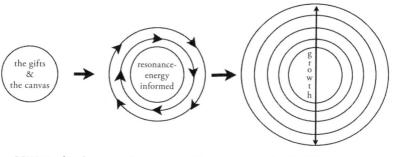

HERE ➜ doing work--meaningful movement ➜ THERE

Figure 24.1. Work done + growth = wellth

Well, what is a bigger investment than your skills and your time? Why wouldn't you think this way about the place you seek employment? Furthermore, why wouldn't everything you do be measured in this way? Relationships? Vacations? Purchases?

World-class performers recognize that everything they do is designed to move them from where they are to where they want to be (see Figure 24.2). The compensation they seek is no exception. If it does not help them do work, if it does not increase their ability to meaningfully move, they don't need it and they don't waste their time pursuing it.

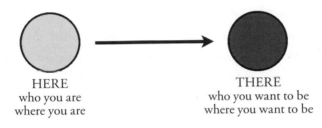

HERE
who you are
where you are

THERE
who you want to be
where you want to be

Figure 24.2. Work is meaningful movement

Consider this from the former International Chairman of Goldman Sachs:

"Title is incidental. Who cares about the title? That's not what you hear out of most corporations. I had a waiting period before I got into grad school. I worked as a management trainee. I went through a lot of departments. When I got to compensation and the personnel department, I spent several weeks. I got to study the compensation of people. I had access to info that most people did not have.

So here's three or four people at the very top making a lot of money. A sea of people who might have worked there for years who were hardly making anything. That was my first education as to what the real world was like in a big company. Damned if I want to do that. The odds of making it into that rarified atmosphere was pretty small.

That's one of the things that has gotten way out of whack in this country. Couple of guys making a hundred million dollars and everybody else swimming around down here with nothing. There has to be a lot of thought to the meritocratic work conditions, the way you evaluate people, the way you bring them along, the way you incent them to do things, and the tangible evidence that you indeed have their interest at heart and to pay them accordingly. I like all of that stuff. I enjoyed it. I liked the diversity of what we did. It was a lot of fun. And I made a ton of mistakes."

In this case, well[th] is the combination of getting to do the work, the education, and the financial remuneration among other things. Most people do not look at compensation this way, nor do most companies. Instead, they seem stuck on the treadmill like TV cartoon character George Jetson yelling, "Jane, get me off this crazy thing."

We have a plethora of self-help and management books out there. Gurus and consultants. Seminars and classes and degrees. I've read, taken, attended, even taught these too. Yet it seems far too many of us still see work and compensation as an exchange of time, effort, and skill for money, and we do not really put the money to work for us, but to escape into consumerism.

This is not the doing of work, rather just *working*. No meaningful movement, no growth, no power, no *well[th]*.

I watch while people collect that money and use it to undo the damage they do to their own lives by the careers or jobs they have chosen. You cannot do work powerfully if you have no idea where you are or some idea of where you want to go. Maybe you simply want to go for the ride and see where that takes you. But it helps to know where you are in life relative to where you might like to go.

You cannot define compensation powerfully if you do not know where you want to go or consider the different ways and means there are to get there.

You cannot do work powerfully if you do not grow in the process of doing work. (See Figure 24.3.) You might move from here to somewhere, but you will not be prepared for any change in course. Compensation is not the exchange of one thing for another, of time and effort for money.

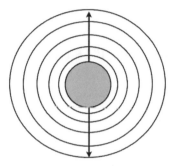

Our increased abilities to use our gifts to inform energy into meaningful movement
Knowing what work is worth doing then being able to do it
The ability to learn from mistakes and failures
To see the unknown as opportunity

Figure 24.3. Growth

Compensation is always the investment of you into your ability to do work and the doing of work in your life and the life of the company. The most powerful form of compensation occurs in the overlaps between individuals and companies or organizations.

As Benjamin Franklin added in the *Declaration of Independence*, "We hold these truths to be self evident." But sometimes as Alfred North Whitehead observed, "It takes an unusual mind to analyze the obvious."

HEAD COACH PHILIPPE AUBERTIN[1]

BEFORE THEY'RE FIT TO BE ON STAGE, ATHLETES HAVE TO REPROGRAM YEARS OF INGRAINED INSTINCTS, SUCH AS MAINTAINING A RIGID POSTURE OR FOCUSING ON SCORES.

---

[1] During the Montreal training sessions, Aubertin tells former athletes that there is no such thing as a perfect 10 in entertainment. *"Losing their 'game faces'."*

Find It

FIND IT

*I*nspiration. Education. Evaluation. Compensation. Combine these into "work" that creates *well*^th^. Well^th^ would be a good thing. Many would argue that wealth would get them to well^th^. For some, perhaps, and for so many, the central focus on the collection of wealth becomes ultimately a frustration. Where does all this take us? If the "haves" make too much more than the "have-nots" and the "haves" also remove all the chances or hope for getting more, eventually, history shows, the "have-nots" will rise up and take it by force. So, it is to the advantage of the "haves" to "share" enough that all can enjoy "life, liberty and the pursuit of happiness." The research data suggest that the "haves" tend not to do that, even among young idealistic students.

Starpower® is an experiential educational simulation that has been around for decades. Almost invariably, the "haves" (predetermined by the luck of the draw) get more and in the end, they make the rules to ensure that they will keep what they have and give only modest, if any, hope to the "have-nots." They won't even communicate with them, but retreat into a privileged environment, and discuss incestuously.

One of my mentors at Harvard, Paul Lawrence and his colleague Nitin Nohria have written a book entitled *Driven* in which they posit that the first of four main instinctive, genetically evolved drives in human beings is to acquire a little bit more.[2] If this is true, then one of the implications

---

[2] The other three are to protect what you have, to mate, and to create.

is that no matter how much someone has, the broad general tendency will be to acquire a little bit more.

I've heard many professionals speak of this as "creating wealth." For the most part, they mean for themselves first and then for those around them in cascading, smaller pieces. One of the implications of this drive would be that in negotiations you'd never want to give more than you absolutely have to because you'd know that the next year, no matter how much they have, "they" will want a little bit more.

At the other end of the spectrum are the rare individuals like the Mid-western road contractor who eventually sold his business for $200 million net. He had a hundred employees. He said that they'd done all the work, so he gave each of them — drivers, secretaries, laborers alike — $1 million each. And kept $100 million.

His argument was, "I have a hundred million, what am I going to do with another hundred million?" Generous. More than fair by today's standards (so many were shocked by his behavior). His logic seems impeccable. How many cars can he buy for $100 million? How many homes? How many trips around the world? Trust funds for his kids? And STILL have a bundle left over for scholarships and endowments. I admire his sense of perspective.

Whatever your perspective or your politics on this issue, the data seem to suggest that money is no guarantee of happiness or of well[th]. I have a shelf of books in my office with titles like *Must Success Cost So Much?*, *The Failure of the American Dream*, *Career Success; Personal Failure* and *The Overworked American*. You can find articles, research, and media stories about the negative effects of winning the lottery. Money doesn't guarantee well[th]. But then neither does poverty. We could easily argue that *some* wealth is essential to some kind of well[th].

Many people get side-tracked from what's truly important and central in life. The world-class performers that Doug interviewed, some 600 of them in at least five different professions, tended to focus more on how they wanted to feel rather than on the immediate results of their work.

This is a big deal because the vast majority of people worldwide seem to have either forgotten or never understood this concept well. How is it that so many get diverted into a focus on results at the expense of internal experience? How do so many of us get side-tracked along the way and begin focusing on doing what "they" want us to do?

I'm sure that school has something to do with it. Sit up straight. Stop poking your neighbor. Do your homework. I'm sure that pre-school has something to do with it. It's a competitive world and I want my child to have a head start. We can't get behind. That's okay, sweetie, be a good girl now and go to school (at age three or four). High school perpetuates the results orientation. You have to get good grades so you can get into a good college! Universities continue the process. You have to get good grades to get a good job. Companies perpetuate the process. Professionals will do what they have to do regardless of how they feel.

SO... if you've lost your feel, or if you have never recognized it, how do you find it (again)? How could one begin to fix this dilemma — the diagonal obstacle barrier shown in Figure 25.1? As I've mentioned, I first encountered all of this at about age 48 so I had basically five decades of habit to try to undo and then reform. Kurt Lewin's old model of managing change — unfreeze, retrain, and refreeze — seems powerfully accurate to me. The unfreezing and the retraining are not as easy as they seem. I've been at it for ten years. Doug tries to get his residents to see it much faster than that. Perhaps I'm a slow learner.

My answer to this question, "How do I find my resonance?" lies in the belief, Doug inspired, that we all have felt this some time, somewhere.

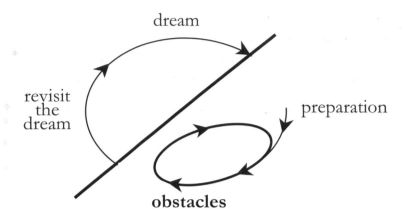

dream

revisit
the
dream

preparation

obstacles

Figure 25.1. Losing your dream

I've confirmed that in my consulting by asking large numbers of people (maybe 2,000+ people over the last nine years) whether they've ever felt *flow*. Virtually everyone says, "Yes." Then you ask them to describe when and where that was and what they were doing to their neighbor and the room bubbles over with energy.

They'll say things like golf, basketball, running, writing code, singing, hiking, flying, working with a team, creating a team-based proposal, building something, and yes, among engineers, even calculus. It's different for everyone. The question is, "What was it for you?"

One technique for finding it, or perhaps re-finding it, then is to reflect with some rigor (by writing it down and revising and polishing it) on the times in your life when you felt flow or resonance or the "zone." Where were you? What were you doing? Most importantly, how did it feel? More than "happy" or "awesome." Find the adjectives. Refine your first draft.

It took me eighteen months of this process to finally boil it down to three words: *light, unhurried* and *engaged.* I feel this when Doug and I send these chapters back and forth. It's the most fun I've had in a long time. In the past, to write, I've made outlines, filled in concepts and then "slogged" through it. Yeoman-like. Disciplined. Like John Steinbeck wrote in his diary when he was writing *The Grapes of Wrath*. He had a daily discipline of 2,500 words, often stopping in mid-sentence. Maybe not always in flow. (Yes, his results were good … but we don't know much about how he was feeling *while* he wrote. He wrote mostly about the other parts of the day. And he must have liked writing well enough to write a diary about his life while he was writing. Hmm?)

See if you can fill in the table in Figure 25.2. Then ponder it and reflect on it and when you've got it "right," that is, when you've got a phrase that describes how you WANT to feel, then the question will be, how can you nurture that on a regular basis. For sure, at least in my experience, this will require unlearning some habits and acquiring some new ones. But if you can do it, my experience is you'll acquire a new kind of well[th].

If you can go through this process — or another — *find* out how you want to feel, then, as my discovery was, you've only just begun. I'd had five decades of habit doing things the results-only way, and I couldn't change them overnight. After *finding* how I wanted to feel, I had to learn how to *nurture* it.

INCIDENTS/ACTIVITIES IN MY PAST WHEN I FELT RESONANCE/FLOW	HOW IT FELT	HOW DO I WANT TO FEEL? (ADJECTIVES)

Figure 25.2. Identifying your resonance

P   O   W   E   R   E   D

MIHALYI CSIKZENTMIHALYI

PEOPLE WHO LEAD A SATISFYING LIFE ARE GENERALLY INDIVIDUALS WHO HAVE LIVED THEIR LIFE ACCORDING TO RULES THEY THEMSELVES CREATED. THEY EAT ACCORDING TO THEIR OWN SCHEDULES, THEY SLEEP WHEN THEY ARE SLEEPY, WORK BECAUSE THEY ENJOY DOING IT, CHOOSE THEIR FRIENDS AND RELATIONSHIPS FOR GOOD REASONS. THEY UNDERSTAND THEIR MOTIVATIONS AND LIMITATIONS. THEY HAVE CARVED OUT A SMALL FREEDOM OF CHOICE.

Sustenance

SUSTENANCE

The people I interviewed almost never talked about being, "in the zone." They were very specific about how they wanted to feel and when they wanted to feel that way. In some cases, they described the way they need to feel to perform. I once heard golfer Retief Goosen described this way. Off the course, when he is not competing, he is very outgoing, even funny. When he competes, he knows he needs to feel calm, even stoic.

Saying you want to be in the zone is the same as saying you want to be happy. It is not enough to be useful. In my experience, people familiar with the concept of *flow* and *the zone*, sometimes use these to pressure themselves, to judge themselves when they cannot get into it. Then they wonder *why* they are not getting into it.

Feel is a skill, a skill we learn to use and develop. It is not a static state we achieve. It is an ongoing dynamic process. We need to develop our ability to feel in order to find the feel we want, recognize it as something different, and then be able to find that feel again.

The better you are at feel, the more you are able use that skill to find the way you want to feel, the chances of getting into the zone increase. The zone is not someplace I want my heart surgeon to be in to perform well. If he gets there, great, but if not I know he can use his skill of feel to be in a good place.

So the first rule of feel is that it is a skill. We follow the feel where it takes us whenever possible. For athletes and surgeons and musicians, this often means practice. I don't mean they have to go to practice, but that they practice in an environment that increases their ability to feel how they want to feel and do what they want to do. Maybe it is shooting baskets or sitting at the drums in a practice room alone. This type of practice leads to preparation because it develops the skill to feel the way they want to feel when they perform. This is more than simply the muscle memory of repetition.

For business people I've interviewed, it means knowing how you want your meetings to feel, how your drive to and from work feels. What do you do when you're stuck in traffic or have a long commute? Do you listen to music? If so do you plan what music you will listen to? Or do you leave that to chance?

Music is one of the most powerful ways to nurture feel, to be able to produce the feel you're looking for. Surgeons I know play certain songs during the toughest parts of the case because it helps them feel the way they need to feel, and they know this from using their skill of feel and listening to it.

Furthermore, how many opportunities do you have to control or influence the environment, the mood, the energy, the feel of your day? I'm certain it is more than you think it is. This is why I have people collect data for me before I work with them. Most people simply are not paying good enough attention to the opportunities.

How often would you eat without having some control over what you ate and how it tasted? How often would you sit in a room and listen to music you can't stand and tell yourself that somehow this is good for you? Yet when it comes to feel this is exactly what people do. They give away these opportunities.

How we feel affects how we perform. So what affects how you feel? Developing your skill of feel simply by using it and paying attention to it will allow you to be a connoisseur of feel in your life. Make a list of what impacts how you feel: sleep, exercise, nutrition, relationships, commuting, the list can go on. You will be amazed how many things in your everyday life you have control over or can influence to create the feel you want.

Many of the business people I interviewed talked about how important it was to them to design their offices and their homes to maximize how they feel everyday. Surgeons I know walk longer routes to the operating room so that they can walk past windows to get some natural light. A best-selling author plays music before and after she writes so she feels the way she wants to feel. One guy who made his first fortune as a systems engineer told me that if you locked him in a room with a computer and Dr. Pepper and leave him alone, he'd be happy for a week.

Artist Robert Irwin compared life to a swing.

> *"It's like you're on a swing and you swing way up to the top and for a split second you can see over the wall, you can see all that light, but you're already on your way back into the world. So you swing harder and you get a little higher and you see a little more, but back down into the world you go. To recognize something and then live there takes a tremendous conversion of your being. You don't just swing up there and say, 'Oh, that's nice,' and stay there, hanging in mid air. Hanging in mid air can be nice ... but the world always draws you back."*

When the world pulls you back down, how do you swing back up again? This is how *feel* works. Maybe someone will come along and give you a push — maybe you even build those people into your life. Other times you will need to push off the ground with your feet again.

World-class performers seem to have figured out how to integrate gravity into their performances. They know they will come down so instead of worrying about it or believing something is wrong, they simply let it happen and then use the energy to swing back up.

A surgeon waiting to do a transplant in the middle of the night might already have had a long, tough day, but she still must perform. She's learned to take power naps, sometimes sleeping in the OR.

Tennis players and golfers swing up for their shots, but they will swing back down in between points or shots. They find a rhythm.

It is not enough to feel the way you want to feel, then try and stay in that place. It is what you do through the entire swing that matters — when you are on the way up, enjoying it while you're in mid air, and then enjoying the downswing and re-energizing the process. It is about momentum, about integrating the different aspects of your life so they feed each other:

This is why *feel* matters so much. At every stage, in every phase, feel informs your needs. Eating, sleeping, exercising all play a part. The role you play in the lives of others, the role they play in yours, all matter.

Probably the greatest threat I have seen in my work to great performance is believing something is wrong when you are on the way down. You might start judging yourself, thinking somehow you are at fault, judging yourself, then pressuring yourself to get back into the "zone." This is one reason I do not use that language when I work with someone.

Knowing how you want to feel, knowing what helps you feel that, allows you to do what you need to do to give yourself a chance. Even the greatest athletes go through slumps and the greatest obstacle they face is pressuring themselves, trying too hard to break out of it. The more they do that, the more they get into their heads and try to control things. If you know the little things, if you focus on them, if you let yourself feel and follow that, it will eventually lead you out of the slump.

Nurturing *feel* requires exactly that. The more detailed your knowledge of what you want to feel, the better informed your energy is.

Allow yourself to find and feel your own rhythm to your life in the same way you would if you were on Irwin's swing. Keep track of it. Do not try to control or create the rhythm. Do the little things, pay attention to the detail, and allow yourself to focus on those. As a basketball player, one thing I learned was that when my shot was not working, didn't feel right, it helped me to focus on playing defense because I could control that. As I focused on that, it loosened me up, and allowed my shot to come back, allowed me to find that feel again.

Sustenance means nutrition and nutrition is all about energy. Without it, the rhythm fades, we become less powerful, and we push too hard. Nurturing means listening to needs and answering their call. It does not mean babying yourself or backing off, but building into the process the things you need.

As we discussed earlier, it means listening and being around others who listen. It means doing work instead of just working or putting in effort or time. It is about rhythm and flow and the acceptance you will not always be in them. It is about being free of judgment, but collecting good data, data that allow for useful evaluation.

What I learned from the people I interviewed was that being world-class demands the skillful use of feel. What I learned from people who struggle is that feel is often the most overlooked and underappreciated aspect of performance and life because it is too often portrayed as selfish. Feel is data — the data that informs energy into flow and rhythm.

HELEN KELLER

THE BEST AND MOST BEAUTIFUL THINGS
IN THE WORLD CANNOT BE SEEN OR EVEN
TOUCHED. THEY MUST BE FELT WITH THE
HEART.

Horsing It,

HORSING IT

*T*he thing for me about rhythm is that I've found myself so many times in life trying to force it. I think this tendency evolved from or emerged from lots of repeated counsel over the years, beginning early in life, that you can do more. It's a concept that is rampant in business — more, more, more. My father once said, I remembered it, "Sometimes you have to horse it." By that he meant sometimes brute force was the only way to go. Looking back on it, whenever I tried to do that, things didn't work out so well.

Deer hunting in the Rockies in Idaho. After days, we see a single deer across a valley, nearly a mile away. Shoot, shoot, shoot. Shooting from frustration more than anything. It's a waste of shells and our frustration dissipates up into the air with the diminishing reverberations of the echoes from the ridge.

School in the mornings — they're doing double shifts because of all the students. Up at six, off to school. Then basketball practice after a two-mile walk to the gym. Then walk home. Then homework. In the second month, I'm walking down the street after practice, and I'm getting dizzy. My vision narrows to a tiny circle the size of a 30.06 barrel. My head is beginning to hurt. My right side does numb — leg, hand, arm, face. Weird. Three days of a splitting headache, any movement, any touch, any light, anything and I'm screaming in pain. They, the migraines, come like clockwork, every 28 days. For six months.

Trying to move an air compressor. It's on wheels. It should move. All I have to do is lift the tongue up a little off the ground and push. Hmm, it's heavier than I thought. But, hey, I'm strong, I have bucked 40–50 pound hay bales six feet over my head. I lift harder. Doesn't budge. Just a little more! I pull harder and I hear a pop and feel this sharp pain in my lower back on the right side. Ruptured disk, L4-L5. It haunts me still.

Doing pushups in my dorm as a freshman. Just a few more. Don't give up now, you maggot! No pain, no gain. More. More. I'm struggling to get up. I see stars. Something pops in my head. I black out briefly. I'm flushed. I have a headache. I lie there for a while, and then gradually am able to sit up. The headache lasts for two days.

Interviewing for a major consulting firm coming out of my MBA program. They tell me I'm near the top of their list. Almost straight As. It looks good, very good. He asks, "How would you handle this?" I search for the theory. I search for the facts. I search for the "right" answer. It doesn't come. The first shall be last.

Overage and single. Missing out on "life." I ask a good-looking woman a year older to go skiing. I borrow my dad's car, front-wheel drive. It's late so we've got to hurry to get to the top of the mountain before they close. The road is snowy. We round a curve trying to make up time, slide through the curve, through the farmer's front fence, and take out his porch. Last date with her.

Being asked to demo a move by my aikido instructor. I thought he was going left. That violates a fundamental principle of aikido, going with the opponent's energy. That anticipation is deadly in the martial arts. He went right. I felt something come loose in my hip. I was on crutches for three weeks.

Changing a flat tire on my car. The lug nut is stuck. I put the wrench on and push. Nothing. I step on it. Nothing. In my head I hear, "When all else fails, horse it." I put my left arm down on the wrench, and push down with all my might. Just a little more and just a little harder. Finally, it gives. But not the lug wrench. Something has given way in my left shoulder. I hear the pop and feel the pain.

Standing on the first tee on the second day of a two-day open golf tournament. I'd shot the round of my life the day before, even par, and now I'm playing with the 'big boys' in the next to the last group. First time ever. I'm hitting fourth. The first three guys all hit nice drives down the middle. It's a wide fairway, stretches off to the right maybe fifty yards wide. I usually hit a fade. I know I can do this. I prepare, go through my routine, swing, way too hard, and it goes dead left into a stand of pine over by the parking lot. We never found it. Double bogey.

We've been up half the night moving boxes. Unloading boxes. Painting. Trying to move in. But I need my exercise. I'm tired, dead tired. My back is tight. I go to the gym anyway. I come down hard. Something pops in that same spot in my back. In the middle of the night, my back spasms, and I'm in excruciating pain. Three days in the hospital.

It's late, been a long day. I've been studying hard. I'm tired. I "need" some exercise. I go over to the gym about 11 pm. I'm wearing an aluminum thumb splint because I got my thumb jammed back on a jump shot earlier in the week. There's only one other guy there so we agree to play one-on-one. Winner's ball. I score. My ball and he needs to check it. In a flash, I decide I'll do a chest pass with spin, land the ball by his foot and have it with English, jump straight up to him. I make the pass, compressing the ball and when my hand comes off the ball, it springs my hand and my splinted thumb jumps into my eye, smack dead center. Ruptured the pupil which fills up with blood. Three days in the hospital, without moving, have to let the tiny blood vessels heal undisturbed.

After working hard, I have one last day in Istanbul. Sleep in. Good breakfast. My black belt test is coming up. I should go to the gym, build up my quads. Aerobic for half an hour. Quad machine. Three sets at max weight. Straining on the last ten reps. Then 120 leg scissors lying on my back. The last 20 were *very* hard to do. I can hear my taekwondo instructor saying, "Don't give up! Don't stop!" When I'm done, I can hardly stand up. Time's short. Go visit the Topkapi Palace. Walk for three hours. Upstairs and down. Massage at the hotel. She's aggressive on my quads, using her elbows. It hurts. Nice dinner. Go out sightseeing. Walking down a flight of stairs, both my quad tendons give way. Lying on the sidewalk, unable to move. It really hurts. How to get home? Twelve days to surgery. Four months before I can walk without aid.

I already told you about how I tried to force it with that large audience once. There are more incidents big and small. Times I tried to force it, horse it. At 48, after eight years of 40 hours a week at work and 40 hours a week in volunteer work, I gave out.

Can you force it? Yes, you can. In my experience, the consequences are usually harsh. At the same time, I see forcing it a lot in the world. Parents who push their kids to school too soon. Who push them to be pro athletes before their time. I see it in business. Managers who push their employees to do more and more and more with less. And then complain when they begin to cut corners. You might get results in the short run. In my experience forcing it, though, is a self-destructive process.

Doug mentioned rhythm at the end of the previous chapter. There is, I think, a rhythm in life. Finding one's rhythm, the *right feel*, like Dave Scott mentioned earlier, is difficult to do amidst all the pressures and expectations from the world outside.

Like the time I tore my right rotator cuff playing hoops and had to clear my calendar — and wrote the third edition to my book. Like the time I was so sick I could hardly walk and shot 73 at St. Andrews. Like the time I got home late from a business trip and had to play with a partner in a tournament and shot even par. In those cases, my body forced *me* to slow down and just execute without thinking too much. My wife thinks it's a pattern in my life. Work hard, too hard, break down and recover. What if I could learn how to do this voluntarily instead of having a broken body demand it?

Stop forcing it. Stop horsing it. Let it flow. Find the rhythm that fits you. Hmm. I can *see* this at Level Two. It's harder to make it happen all the time.

How about you? Do you remember what it was like when, if ever, you were young and *not* pushing? When your life flowed in a seamless harmony with what was going on around you? When you were spontaneous and powerful?

Some kids, not all, seem to have this resonance thing down well. And something happens to most of them. Life, as McCammon wrote, does its best to take that magic away.

JOSEPH CAMPBELL

WHEN YOU FIND AN AUTHOR THAT REALLY GRABS YOU, READ EVERYTHING HE HAS DONE. JUST READ WHAT THIS ONE AUTHOR HAS TO GIVE YOU AND THEN YOU CAN GO READ WHAT HE HAD READ. AND THE WORLD OPENS UP IN A WAY THAT IS CONSISTENT WITH A CERTAIN POINT OF VIEW. BUT WHEN YOU GO FROM AUTHOR TO AUTHOR, YOU MAY BE ABLE TO TELL US THE DATE WHEN EACH WROTE SUCH AND SUCH A POEM — BUT HE HASN'T SAID ANYTHING TO YOU.

PHYSICS

*J*oseph Campbell once wrote that the best way to learn is to read something you like then follow the trail of the author's influences, read what the author read. I've spent the last few years reading about physics because of a long drive I took with friends. Between Los Angeles and Vancouver British Columbia, we listened to Bill Bryson's *A Short History of Nearly Everything.*

Because of Bryson, the most recent additions to my personal library have been books by Richard Feynman, Albert Einstein, Stephen Hawking, Brian Greene, and some other lesser known physicists.

While I cannot claim I understand physics, the language they use provides me a new way of seeing what I heard in my interviews with world-class performers. Their language is, as Brian Greene says in *The Elegant Universe,* elegant — as powerful as it is simple.

Their vocabulary introduced me to simple explanations of work, force, energy, power, resonance, velocity, and more. These were ideas I'd heard in more abstract terms when I listened to world-class performers and I was hearing them more clearly when I heard them in physics terms.

Take for example the topic of *force:* doing work, moving something from here to there. Isn't that what we are all trying to do? Move ourselves, our families, our companies from where we are to where we think we want to

be. That could almost define leadership, helping people move from one place to a better place.

If we're doing work, we want to do it with power, where the benefit-cost ratio favors the benefit with the least amount of cost. If we use force, we want to apply the force that costs us the least and gets the most work done.

The people I interviewed all approached their lives and their careers in this elegant manner. They valued doing *work* over *working*. They measured their power not by putting others down, but by how effectively they were able to move from where they were to where they wanted to be. In most cases they took others with them to the benefit of all. I know this because part of my research included talking to other people in the lives of the world-class performers.

Residents at the University of Virginia medical school singled out one heart surgeon who treated them as family, who made sure they learned how to *care* about people as well as *take care* of them. A CEO's secretary told me her boss made her education a priority so she could advance her own career and provide more for her daughters. Musicians and athletes who worked with the world-class performers I had interviewed said the performers made them better simply by being in their lives, modeling how to do work, how to excel in a way that passed on something special to the next generations. A professional poker player bought drove to every major sporting event in the country raising money for cancer in honor of his aunt who died.

I had no interest in physics as a discipline when I was younger, however as an athlete, my life was all about physics. How do I make the ball move through the hoop? How do I pitch a ball with the most speed and the least effort? How do I run the fastest using the least amount of energy? I just hadn't realized this was what physics is.

Now this perspective informs what I do. As I help people consider their life's work, the information they use, their own power to do work, I help them define work on their own terms.

I don't mean to oversimplify physics. I am just saying that the more I read, the more I see the stories of the people I interviewed in physics terms.

Even work and energy can be talked about this way. Seth Lloyd in *Programming the Universe* wrote:

> *"Ultimately, information and energy play complementary roles in the universe: Energy makes physical systems do things. Information tells them what to do. The maximum rate at which a physical system can process its information is proportional to its energy. Earth, air, fire, and water in the end are all made of energy, but the different forms they take are determined by information. To do anything requires energy. To specify what is done requires information."*

So much of my work is about the effective match between your information and your energy. This can mean the difference between average and great, between mundane and world-class. When information does not inform our energy to do work powerfully or with elegance, performers fall flat.

Most of us have heard of the Peter Principle where we reach our level of incompetence. My experience, however is we reach the point where the fit between or energy and information simply do not fit. I hear this most often in my consulting when I see the friction between the money people and the mission people. Worst of all is when the mission people, the true believers get promoted to the point where they are disconnected from the daily experience of the work the do for their members or clients or even their families. I've seen surgeons stop operating and teaching to become administrators, teachers and coaches take promotions that remove them from the field or the classroom where they thrived. I've seen pilots and athletes stop flying or stop playing to become teachers simply because they had no idea what else to do.

Another way to think about this is as positive and negative energy. Positive energy is energy transferred in a way that gets work done. Positive energy is energy informed and expended in moving us from where we are to where we want to go. Negative energy is energy expended that gets no work done. Negative energy is energy expended that results in no movement or work and worse can cause long-term damage.

Suppose you want to move a television from the street up to a third floor apartment. You carry the television up the stairs. You get it to the door of your apartment. You rest it on the railing. As you reach to open the door, it falls over the railing and rolls all the way down.

You expended energy and the television is back on the first floor, now probably in a thousand pieces. No forward movement was made, nothing accomplished, but energy has been expended. Even worse, you will probably beat yourself up, judge yourself negatively, and expend even more energy that gets nothing done.

In every company I worked with and on every team I was on, I saw two kinds of people — those who did work, who expected to be evaluated on the work they did and those who simply worked (expended energy) but did little to move the company from here to there.

So many of us are told that *hard work matters*. We judge ourselves too often by how hard we worked and not often enough by the work we actually do. When we feel like we've put out maximum effort, we want to be acknowledged for that, even when someone who seemed to work less hard actually moved the ball down the field.

As we grow up, it's easy to allow ourselves to define our work in a way that gains the approval of people we care about. Parents, coaches, teachers, friends. We allow others to define the work we come to believe is worth doing. Good grades, good colleges, good jobs, nice houses, 2.5 kids. We allow people to define not only what success is, but also the path to that success. In this place, people burnout or simply never get where they want to go. Energy expended with little work done.

Even some of the world-class performers I interviewed went through this at one time. Fame crept in and corrupted the purity of their skill in what they did. They chased things outside of themselves. They became lonely and isolated.

The people who made it through that place are the ones who had an awakening, a re-examination of their life's work. The musicians who make it over the long run might have started their careers in order to meet women, but over time they fall in love with music. Doctors who might have become doctors because that is what they were told would make them successful, fall in love with taking care of their patients.

We learn how to inform energy into doing work. We learn the skill of doing this in the same way we learn the skill of feel. The more we actually do our life's work, the more we fulfill our own promise, we end up helping more people. And in the end we please more people by doing our own life's work.

Feel matters in all of this because our uninformed energy wells up inside of us and wants to burst.

Do you expend energy by going to work and getting a paycheck and getting through the days or do you inform your energy and do work that moves your life powerfully in the direction you want to go?

One musician I interviewed told me his philosophy is to be the best musician he could be, to be the "baddest," and at times it's hard to get along with others while he is trying to do that. I hear this conflict all the time. It is this conflict that leads to negative energy — the need for approval of others, people who may have invested in our success, but then who are offended when we need to let go of them or suggest they don't really understand.

In most cases, the ability of world class performers to feel what they felt informed their energy. They allowed themselves to be judged based on their performance only when the judgment included useful information and could help them improve. They were willing to abandon ineffective ways of doing work to pursue better ways. The judgment didn't create doubt, rather better work.

Richard Feynman talks about doubt, something many of us consider negative, as positive energy. He wrote that one of the greatest values of science is the freedom to doubt. Freedom allows us to reconsider, to change course, to wonder instead of worry. Doubting that the work you are doing or how you are doing it is powerful or meaningful can be very freeing, allowing you to find new and better ways to inform your energy.

In the book, *Defining the Wind*, Scott Huler even links this with feel:

> "...our own body is the greatest perceptive instrument ever designed. Not only can it perceive sound, light, movement, temperature, aroma, taste, and time, but it possesses all the processing capacity and speed to organize, categorize, and express that mass of data almost instantly, to then retain and reorganize it, and to find utility and value and meaning."

Jackie Joyner Kersee, who battled severe asthma, and still won six Olympic Medals said:

> *I think the reason I like jumping is it is like being free. I like freedom. I like being able to do what I feel.*

BY Y F E E L

ED VIESTURS, *VOICES OF THE SUMMIT*

THE WESTERN MAN DOESN'T WANT TO LEARN HOW TO CLIMB, HE ONLY WANTS TO GET TO THE TOP. THE PURPOSE OF RISKING YOUR NECK IN AN ADVENTURE IS TO ATTAIN SOME SORT OF SPIRITUAL OR PERSONAL GROWTH. THIS WILL NOT HAPPEN IF YOU ARE SO FIXATED ON THE GOAL THAT YOU COMPROMISE THE PROCESS ALONG THE WAY.

Numbers Game

NUMBERS GAME

*B*y chance, I'm reading Carl Sagan's *Pale Blue Dot* as Doug sends his chapter on physics. There are a lot of numbers in the book — even though it's written for the lay person. The numbers representing the distances in the cosmos, the probabilities of life, the sizes, the length of light waves and radar waves, are so beyond our daily experience they are hard to comprehend. Mastering the numbers is critical to understanding space.

Executives would say the same thing about understanding business; you need to know the numbers. Executives, most of them, want to do real work. They want to get things done. They use numbers to communicate what they've done. And, given the way that the story the numbers tell affects so many others, sometimes they report what they *wanted* the numbers to say.

I remember one client. I had interviewed the guys working on the shipping dock. They told me that they did some odd things around there.

"Like what," I said.

"Like shipping next quarter's orders this quarter."

It was near the end of the quarter, so what appeared to be happening was the company was striving to make its quarterly numbers by shipping next quarter's orders a bit earlier.

When do you count sales? When the order comes in? When they leave the dock? When the end user pays the bill? (My accounting friends have many answers for these questions.)

An hour later I was in the CEO's office for a scheduled meeting. I noted in passing that it seemed that the company was shipping orders early in order to make its current numbers.

"We don't do that."

"Hmm. I was just down there talking with the guys on the dock, and they say it's happening."

The CEO wasn't alarmed, didn't seem interested in going down to check it out. He just repeated, "We don't do that."

Six months later I heard that sales dropped 60 percent in one month. Can you imagine how dry the mouths went and how tight the sphincters went when they heard that report? It turned out that 50 percent of their shipments went to a captive wholesaler. Finally, the wholesaler called them up and said, "Hey, we can't store your finished goods inventory anymore! Our warehouses are full!"

But the company had been counting those shipments as sales. They were playing a numbers game and the numbers didn't reflect what was *really* taking place. As far as anyone reading the report was concerned, sales looked strong. But the reality was the product was not selling at the end of the supply chain. Management wasn't being held accountable for product in the supply chain — only for what they "sold."

In many ways, this numbers game is understandable. Wall Street analysts (many of whom have never run anything) demand monotonically increasing sales and profits reports. As long as that happens, a company's stock price will tend to rise. So, bad things happen when key indicators like sales and profits go down. People stop buying your stock. Your ability to raise capital goes down. Your ability to borrow may decline. You may lose your annual performance bonus. If the CEO has a performance contract that specifies a percent increase in indicators like sales, profits, and/or stock price, it's natural to pull out all the stops so the numbers show what you want them to show.

If you're in a large corporation, your boss's annual review may depend on your producing these monotonically increasing numbers. The pressure on you from your boss to produce those numbers would be high. It's largely a numbers game.

The same is true in many endeavors, especially after the birth of the scientific method and the Industrial Revolution. People want more and more to be "rational" and to rely on facts not feelings. Data. Numbers. There is a way though that the numbers don't tell the whole story and in fact may be quite deceiving. Even if your work is highly visible.

Like running a marathon. They can watch you, publicly, much more closely than the shipping procedures at a subsidiary. They can see if you're cutting (literal) corners. Unless you're Rosey Ruiz. Remember Rosey? She took the subway while running the New York Marathon and came across the finish line first. Her results numbers were great. But somehow, they were too good. They checked. She'd cut corners. The numbers didn't tell the whole story.

Doing work or working (to use Doug's distinction) in a large corporation is not so visible. Individuals in France or Hong Kong can and have virtually destroyed large corporations by making small numbers in a quiet way. Managers at Enron, Worldcom, Adelphia Cable, and Tyco moved the numbers around a little so that the results didn't tell the whole story. Along the way the numbers for those companies looked good.

Tim Gallwey, author of the *Inner Game* series of books, notes that if you measure a thing, people tend to pay attention to it. What an understatement! If you measure a manager on quarterly sales, he or she will feel pressure to make those numbers and do everything they can to make them. Is it dishonest, immoral, unethical, or illegal to do so? Society says only when you cross a certain line, a moving

> It ALL boils down, at some point, to feel.

target. How much does one report as tax-deductible business expenses? Do you deduct a home office? Do you use the company car for personal use? What do the numbers say and how do they match up with the reality?

Does the number of miles you logged last week indicate your health? If you can do 100 pushups are you "strong?" If you write 15 books, are you smart? If you sell 1,000,000 records are you a good singer? If you have a gazillion dollars in the bank, will you be happy?

It ALL boils down, at some point, to feel.

If jogging doesn't make you feel good, what good is it? If going to work doesn't make you feel good, what good is it? If you have a new car, and you don't feel good, what good is it? If you are rich and you don't feel good, what good is it?

The problem I often see around me (and in me) is this notion that "If and when I get ... I'll feel better." Dawn Staley, one of Doug's interviewees, captured it very well. She noted that while she has a goal to win and to get the Gold Medal, that's not why she plays. She plays, she said for the feeling she gets when she's in the game, it's near the end of a tight game, she's playing against the world's best competition, and she's got the ball. That *feeling*, she says, is what brings her back again and again.

It's a cliché to say "it's the journey not the destination." The cliché though is too broad, and too general and if you're dismissing the discussion with, "Oh, yeah, that," beware. The cliché is true, *and* it's much deeper than that.

Here's the point: we're not saying you should give up on goals, numerical milestones of progress. What we are saying is that unless you realize and manage your life and your organization with an equal and balanced emphasis on feel along with goals, you'll be driving toward mediocrity.

Working without feel tends to create working without doing work and a loss of energy. Working without goals can be aimless and consumptive. The world-class approach is to pay attention to feel first, primarily, and then focus that energy toward a goal. But the primary goal is how you want to feel, not just what you want to do. Doing the reverse drains energy and creates organizations full of mediocrity.

Consider this excerpt from Maurice Herzog, the first man to climb an 8,000 meter peak. This occurred in 1952 a year before Norgay and Hillary summited Everest:

> "...we still had a long way to go. Like ants getting over an enormous obstacle we climbed up without appearing to make any progress. The slope was very steep.... The air was luminous, and the light was tinged with the most delicate blue. On the other side of the couloir, ridges of bare ice refracted the light like prisms and sparkled with rainbow hues. The weather was still set fine — not a single cloud — and the air was dry. I felt in splendid form and as if, somehow, I had found a perfect balance within myself — was this, I wondered, the essence of happiness."
>
> Maurice Herzog, *Annapurna*, p. 166

Notice that Herzog realized that summiting was not the ultimate thing. Clearly it was a goal, AND he notes that he's experiencing the ultimate thing 8,000 feet from the summit. Standing on top, many mountaineers report that their central thought is, "Get me down off this damn mountain."

When I ask practicing managers when they've felt flow/resonance, they talk about a lot of different things, some work-related, some not. While some will mention a project team they worked on for days or months, they have never said, "Reading the quarterly results." According to Peter Senge, Deming (the US statistician who founded the total quality movement in Japan) once said that you can measure only 3% of what really matters. When you realize your goal, the ultimate thing, the *feel*, is over. (See Figure 29.1.) Do you realize that? If not, you may be playing a numbers game to the detriment of what really matters. The *more-is-better* numbers game is dangerous. The real definition of success is not in the numbers — the bank account, the fame, the power. Real success is when it felt so good, you want to do it again! The numbers will follow that.

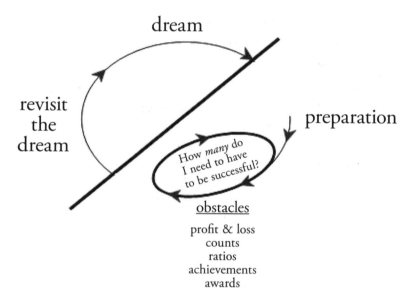

Figure 29.1. The numbers game

LEWIS CAROL, *ALICE IN WONDERLAND*

'THE QUESTION IS,' SAID ALICE, 'WHETHER YOU CAN MAKE WORDS MEAN SO MANY DIFFERENT THINGS.' 'THE QUESTION IS,' SAID HUMPTY DUMPTY, 'WHICH IS TO BE MASTER — THAT'S ALL.'

Master of the

MASTER OF THE NUMBERS

*R*ight after reading Jim's chapter on the numbers game for the first time, I watched on TV people climbing up a face of K2 that had not been climbed before. On the way up, one man died. On the way down, another one died.

This is analogous to achieving goals as a way of measuring one's life. If you reach the goals you set, but in the process sacrifice health or maybe even your life, how good of a goal is it? Is achieving it worth your effort?

I don't judge goals other people go after, but I do wonder about the process by which they chose. This is at the heart of my work. Does the process you use to create goals serve you well? Too many people would answer this question, "No," and too often they realize it too late in life.

In *American Mania*, author Peter Wheybrow offers perspective on capitalism from Adam Smith. Wheybrow suggests that three components define capitalism as described by Smith. Those three are self-love, curiosity, and ambition.

Self-love is learning, knowing, and doing what is in your interest. This extends to the people you care about, specifically your family. By paying attention to their needs you look out for your legacy.

Numbers

Curiosity, the wonder of why and how things work, is a call, a desire to find things out, to take risk, to invent.

Ambition, Wheybrow suggests, is the pursuit of social status.

For each individual, these three work together to move us from where we are to who we want to be. One might be stronger than the other in each of us, though, and sometimes out of balance. The belief in a free market economy suggests that market forces will teach us a lesson, reward us when these are done well, and punish us when they are not. The more we listen to these individual characteristics, the more we can respond, adjust and hopefully adapt. If we have children, we pass those lessons along.

The difficulty comes when a society, the culture in which we live, embraces or rejects one aspect of this at the expense of others. My own observation is that the pendulum swings too often and too far in the direction of someone else's ambition at the cost of our self-love and curiosity. We do what we need to do to survive socially. That does not define self-love and is no friend to curiosity. Our survival is too often defined outside-in.

The world-class performers I interviewed could be described as capitalists under Wheybrow's explanation. They loved themselves enough to learn, know, and do what allowed them to be healthy, physically and emotionally, not all the time, but often enough:

They were curious. How do I make this guitar *talk*? How do I sell this new program? How do I make the ball go in the hoop? They balanced wonder with doubt.

They were ambitious. They often talked about wanting to be the best. Musicians talked about wanting to meet girls, to be socially acceptable even though they did not excel in sports or in the classroom. They wanted nice things. They did not depend on these things alone, however, to make them feel how they wanted to feel.

What they rarely did was to choose one of these three characteristics at the expense of another. And when they did, they listened to the data that highlighted their digression. They listened to how they felt.

They knew that ignoring one of these had consequences. Stop loving yourself or acting in your best interests and you risk illness. Stop wondering and you fall behind and are left only to follow others to *their* ideas, you stop improving in the direction of your dreams. Lose ambition and you find yourself stuck where you are.

This works in the other direction as well. Be too selfish and you'll find yourself alone and isolated. Be too curious and you'll stop working because you'll spend too much time in your head with little or no work being done. Be too ambitious and while you might gain a lot of social status, no one will care about you for anything other than your money and possessions.

When I read Wheybrow and then Adam Smith, I heard the words of my interviewees in what they wrote. What I heard was that all three are defined at least partly by *feel*. And, they are susceptible to being hijacked by that accumulation of outside-in voices we carry inside our heads.

A *New York Times* columnist wrote about the need of curiosity, wonder, and imagination:

> "If you look at Einstein's major theories — special relativity, general relativity and the quantum theory of light — "all three come from taking rebellious imaginative leaps that throw out old conventional wisdom," Mr. Isaacson said. "Einstein thought that the freest society with the most rebellious thinking would be the most creative. If we are going to have any advantage over China, it is because we nurture rebellious, imaginative free thinkers, rather than try to control expression.
>
> We have to remind our kids ... that a math equation or a scientific formula is just a brush stroke the good Lord uses to paint one of

the wonders of nature," Mr. Isaacson said, "And we should look at it as being as beautiful as art or literature or music." My favorite quotation is that "imagination is more important than knowledge." A society that restricts imagination is unlikely to produce many Einsteins — no matter how many educated people it has. But a society that does not stimulate imagination when it comes to science and math won't either — no matter how much freedom it has."

As a result, we are left with ambition and a steady diet of books and courses and marketing that define social status for us. We listen to those around us who tell us, judge us, based on ambition. Then we come back to the idea of potential instead discovering and learning and knowing the promise inside each of us. We are no longer masters of our own domain.

I heard in my interviews how often performers were told they could never succeed, were not good enough. In short, they were being too ambitious.

What I heard in my interviews could be confused with this way of thinking and I had to dig to really understand. These world-class performers had useful dreams and goals, useful in that they inspired meaningful movement. Their dreams and goals *did work* for them. They either moved forward or they grew because of their dreams and goals. And as they got better they learned how goals and dreams worked together to produce movement forward and growth simultaneously.

Each time Jeff Rouse broke the world record for the 100 meter backstroke, he got out of the pool thinking how easy it had been, how swimming with easy speed left him knowing he could go faster. He told me after one swim he realized he could go under 53 seconds, and because of how he felt coming out of the pool after the race, he truly believed it. This was a dream and goal coming together to do work, of a goal set from the inside out. His *number* had meaning because of how he felt when he swam.

Numbers are too often viewed as a measure that leads to judgment of ourselves or others. For the people I interviewed, numbers were just data that led to curiosity, to wonder. How can I be better? What did I miss?

In other words, numbers are data that inform energy to do work. Maybe the numbers tell us where we are and we use that to make decisions about where want to go, to produce useful goals and dreams that inspire work, meaningful movement. Maybe they baffle us and we scratch our heads and wonder how that could be? That wonder leads to questions and doubt about what we've been doing. Maybe they are better then expected and we wonder what we did by accident (this happens a lot in my work) that we could learn to do on purpose. Maybe the numbers tell us we were not ambitious enough or overshot, leading us to reconsider what social status we truly want or how to get there.

When I was getting my graduate degree, I was struck by the split between the quantitative and qualitative academics. It was almost war between them. I wondered why you could not be both. What I found in doing both was that the numbers gave me one set of information, but by itself was useless. In the words and interviews (qualitative) I found processes and results. The qualitative taught me things I did not know that I had not even thought to ask about. In the quantitative, I found ways of testing what I thought I knew. When the numbers came back, when they baffled me, I'd look at my methodology to see if I made a mistake, which was too often the case. But I also went back to my assumptions and sought wisdom from others about their experiences and processes.

When I played sports, when I sold software, numbers had their place. In high school I was the sixth leading score on my team as a junior — yet I was the MVP of the team. I learned early that numbers only held the meaning I gave them. When I sold software, the best guys in the company never seemed to care about the numbers. They cared about their relationships with their clients. The numbers took care of themselves.

How do you decide which numbers have meaning in your life? Based on the pressures of the world, of masters, how does that inform your energy to do work? Do the numbers in your life make you afraid?

Performers give meaning to the numbers of their lives in ways that inspire the doing of work. They know what they want or are at least in the ballpark. If they are wrong, if something more compelling reveals itself, they move on ... and their energy is usually informed by what they feel.

Numbers are like words. They have meaning and they have the power you give them. It is that meaning that informs energy, not the numbers themselves. You may never be master of the universe but you can master the numbers of your life.

KEN LAY, FORMER CEO OF
ENRON[1]

I'VE NOT ONLY PURSUED THE AMERICAN
DREAM, I'VE ACHIEVED IT. I SUPPOSE WE
COULD SAY THE LAST FEW YEARS, I'VE ALSO
ACHIEVED THE AMERICAN NIGHTMARE.

---

[1] Response to questioning from his lawyer George Secrest.

Triangle Trade

TRIANGLE TRADEOFFS

The expedition that summited K2 in the summer of 2007 led by Chris Warner was the most successful summit summer on K2 ever. K2 is far more deadly than Everest proportionately yet that summer, 22 people reached the top. Many seasons *no one* successfully summits K2. I know this because, by coincidence, we are writing a case[2] on the K2 expedition. Doug didn't know that. Chris Warner came to our studios at the invitation of one of his team members, a former student of mine, Joel Shalowitz.

The K2 2007 story is a remarkable one. Chris was able to organize a coalition of several different national teams to bring together a collage of resources that individually did not exist and would have made the summit attempts even more dangerous than they were. The Russians were strong climbers. Others had more rope. Others tents and equipment. And Chris' ability to manage across cultures helped significantly to make the combined effort truly world-class and successful. He also had a quality of character that made him choose to "sweep the mountain," that is, be the last man down to ensure that no one was left behind.

It takes many things to make a successful summit bid of an 8,000 meter peak: resources, talent, leadership, and luck among them. And as Doug mentioned in the previous chapter, if you over-compromise on any one, the success of the whole is threatened.

---

[2] A "case" is a description of a problem used for educational purposes in medicine, law, and business.

This brings to mind challenges that business executives and managers struggle with, how to make those tradeoff decisions. I see it in individual lives as well, the struggle to balance work and family and personal life. Much has been written about binary tradeoffs — costs and revenues, innovation and sticking-to-your-knitting, growth and attending to current operations. In fact most executives and individuals have to make tradeoffs among multiple competing forces.

Let's consider for a moment triangle tradeoffs where there are three competing forces that are demanding attention. Karl Weick[3] has highlighted a classic triangle tradeoff: speed, cost and quality. The premise is that if you try to increase your speed, this costs more and may compromise your quality. If you try to increase your quality, this usually costs more and may slow down your speed. If you try to reduce your costs, you may experience reductions in quality and speed. Figure 31.1 shows this triangular tradeoff visually.

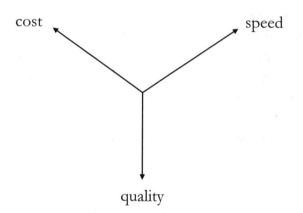

cost   speed

quality

Figure 31.1. Triangle tradeoffs

---

[3] Karl Weick, *The Social Psychology of Organizing*, Addison-Wesley, Reading, MA, 1969.

Modern lean management theory suggests that you can have in organizations all three, high levels of speed and quality and low levels of cost. Nevertheless, it's a challenge to create those conditions.

In the self leadership realm, that is, in managing your own life, many people find it a challenge to get the balance they want in life. Further, many aren't even clear *what* balance they want.

I've developed a *Balance Wheel* exercise that helps people see what their current balance in life might be. The idea is that we all have various "— al" aspects of life and that these aspects are there whether we pay attention to them or not. These dimensions include the physical, the intellectual, the social, the financial, the material, the emotional, and so forth. See Figure 31.2.

When we're born, our development on any of these — AL dimensions is close to zero represented by the center of the diagram. Over time, by the circumstances in which we live and the choices we make, we develop — or not — on each of these dimensions. We'll scale the concentric rings from zero to ten. So, ten — the ourter ring — represents "world class" on that dimension. On the physical dimension, world-class would mean a world record holder or an Olympic Gold Medalist. On the financial dimension, world-class would mean Carlos Slim of Mexico, Bill Gates of the United States, or the Sultan of Brunei. And so on.

The related questions then are "What's your level of development thus far in life?" "How far, given your age, have you developed so far?" "In which, if any, of these dimensions are you striving for excellence (world-class)?" The profile in Figure 31.2 represents an individual in a case we often teach. You can review it to get the idea of how we humans develop over time — and that we don't develop evenly across all dimensions.

You could use this profile to assess your level of development periodically, say annually, to "see" how your personal profile is growing — or not.

The next question would be "what do you *want* your profile to look like?" Your ideal personal profile is represented by the thick black line in Figure 31.2. In some areas, you may be right where you want to be. In other areas, you may have gaps, areas for further development. With this information you could begin to choose what you wanted to do with your time and energy to enhance your development as time passes.

Jim Collins in his book, *Good to Great*, proposes what he calls the "hedgehog concept" as a key ingredient for an individual or an organization to move from good to great, from mediocre to world-class. His point is that individuals and organizations need to focus their energies in order to get good at something. My colleague, Alex Horniman, often says, "Excellence is a neurotic lifestyle." The natural corollary of this is that a *circle* on the diagram in Figure 31.2 is *not* the goal. No one is likely to be world-class at multiple things. Excellence requires a focus, like the hedgehog.

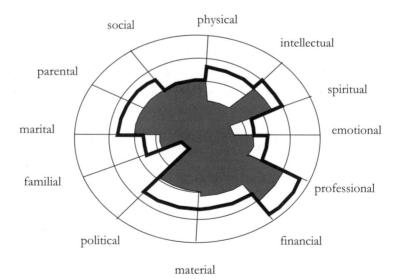

Figure 31.2. A personal developmental balance wheel

We could diagram Collins' hedgehog concept as shown in Figure 31.3 — another triangular tradeoff between passion, talent, and economic viability. Collins asserts, and I agree with him, that it's at the intersection of those three elements where world-class performance is born.

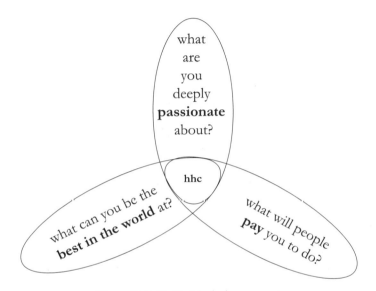

Figure 31.3. Collins' hedgehog concept

You could argue that in a purist view of the world, you don't need to be paid to experience world-class performance. In that world, it's the experience of the performance whether others see it, believe it, or pay for it or not. As Doug argued in the previous chapter, if you perform at your best, the rewards, the results, the numbers will take care of themselves. Mastering the numbers ironically is about focusing on *feel* and letting others do the measuring.

For our purposes here, we suggest that if you want to experience world-class performance, the way to do that is to pay more attention to how you balance your efforts (energy) in life. Consider the triangular tradeoff

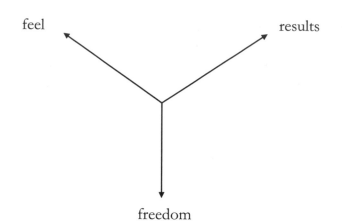

feel   results

freedom

Figure 31.4. Triangle tradeoffs with feel

shown in Figure 31.4. Here we show tradeoffs between feel, results and freedom. Managers who believe in the "professionals will do what they have to do regardless of how they feel" assumption discussed earlier will tend to emphasize results at the expense of freedom and feel. People who overemphasize feel may not pay attention enough to results and might reduce their freedoms (e.g. short-term counterfeits like alcohol, drugs, outside-in thrills, and actors who cannot find stage work and have to support themselves as waiters). People who overemphasize freedom may not be able to support themselves.

Many managers focus just on results. In so doing, they underemphasize the importance of feel and freedom. In the diagram, there would be a medium vector on results and short vectors on feel and freedom. People who have low energy and feel obligated to do what they do tend to produce, again ironically, fewer results (see Figure 31.5).

To master the numbers, people need to be able to find the right tradeoffs — in their personal lives and in their professional lives. People who emphasize feel and freedom tend to produce major results, long vectors, on all legs.

feel   results

freedom

Figure 31.5. Overemphasis on results

Finding the right tradeoffs, the razor's edge of the snow covered ridge on the way to the summit, is a challenge. If one missteps to the left or right, one might tumble thousands of feet to an untimely death. If one misjudges where the center of the trail should be given the deceiving appearance of the snow cornices, the footing may give way and one falls through. On K2 or Everest, these decisions are critical to immediate survival and success. In life, and in management, the results may not be so immediate, but the consequences can be equally devastating.

Are you paying attention to how you want to feel? Or have you long since put that aside? Are you paying attention to your balance between freedom and obligation? Or are you spending your life doing mostly what you "have" to do? Are you focused entirely on measurable results — or have you learned along the way to find, nurture, and protect how you want to feel? Have you found a way to make those triangular tradeoffs? Is it serving you well?

WALT WHITMAN, *LEAVES OF GRASS*

YOU SHALL NO LONGER TAKE THINGS AT
SECOND OR THIRD HAND ...
NOR LOOK THROUGH THE EYES OF THE
DEAD ...
NOR FEED ON THE SPECTRE IN BOOKS,
YOU SHALL NOT LOOK THROUGH MY EYES
EITHER, NOR TAKE THINGS FROM ME,
YOU SHALL LISTEN TO ALL SIDES AND FILTER
THEM FROM YOURSELF.
NOT I, NOT ANYONE ELSE, CAN TRAVEL
THAT ROAD FOR YOU,
YOU MUST TRAVEL IT FOR YOURSELF.

FREEDOM

*W*ork is meaningful movement, from here to there, from where you are to where you want to be. You supply or define the meaning of that movement. That meaning is impacted or influenced or even defined by how and what you feel.

Most of us join, need, or seek out organizations, groups, teams, and so on to help us do the work of our lives. Many of us, join, need, or seek out others because part of doing our work is to help others succeed in doing the work of their lives.

Everything I do, everything I've written to this point is about the possible role *feel* plays in the doing of work, of meaningful movement, as was communicated to me in my experiences with others. I've primarily learned this from two sources — the world-class performers I've been fortunate enough to interview and the people with whom I've shared what I learned through consulting, one-on-one work, and presentations.

The final piece of this is finding as many different ways as possible to communicate what I've learned so the people I share with actually understand me. I read books, watch movies, listen to people, try new things as often as I can. When I do this well, when there is a good fit, energy is informed into meaningful movement or the doing of work. Mine and the people I share with.

Everyone I share with brings a different perspective, different experiences, different feelings to the process. My job, my responsibility, my joy is to inform their energy into the doing of work, their work, as best I can. If this means referring someone to another consultant, to a physician, to someone better than me, it is my duty to do so.

One area at the heart of all human existence and therefore the heart of feel is *freedom*. The purpose of my work is increasing the freedom others have in bringing meaning to their work and the *skills to do their work*. This freedom is so important because at the end of the day, people must own their decisions and their consequences. What I do impacts the lives of others, sometimes greatly.

As someone who works in the medical field, seeing life and death decisions made each day, let me steal a line from medicine. I believe in *informed consent*, information provided so people can make good decisions.

Early on in developing a consulting relationship, people tell me that when something happens to them, they will ask themselves, "I wonder what Doug would say?" Sometimes they tell me that proudly as if they understand what I am sharing with them. Nothing could be further from the truth.

When they say that, I know they do not understand. That's outside-in. I want them to say to themselves, "What do I want to do or how do I feel about this?" I want them to have the skills to answer those questions. And herein lies the trap of coaching.

We love coaches, respect them, believe they have our best interests at heart. We might even put them on a pedestal unfairly. We might expect too much of them.

But here's the thing. Being a coach can be incredibly powerful. What you coach people to know, to do, to believe can last their entire lives. If they care about you, if they love you and respect you, unlearning or letting go of what you teach them can be incredibly difficult. And yet this is exactly what defines great coaches.

In my interviews with world-class performers, they often said that a coach taught them one thing. They taught these performers to believe in their possibilities, their abilities to discover and learn. They might have taught them to despise losing and failing, but they did not teach them to fear losing or failing.

Coaching is about freedom. Your job is to increase the freedom of others and in doing so, you increase your freedom. I wrote my dissertation on freedom and its perceived role in performance. That led me to interview these world-class performers. I learned about freedom from these interviews and the importance of living free.

Helping others has made me free to help even more people in ways I could never have imagined, could never have accomplished if I held onto trying to be seen as an expert, afraid to show I am learning as much as I am giving.

What I heard, learned from, business people, athletes and coaches and many others at the top of their field, made me realize that part of being world-class is *inner* freedom. As Albert Einstein once said, "Inner freedom is an infrequent gift of nature and a worthy object for the individual." My experiences lead me to see this inner freedom is an important aspect of world-class performance. Lack of it prevents people from moving forward.

I've listened while executives teared up about their fear of being judged as inadequate. I've had late-night phone conversations with collegiate coaches worried about their status after a big or surprising loss. I've worked into the early morning hours with successful people wanting to walk away from their success in search of their own definition, yet too frightened of others to ever make the change. I saw and heard and felt a difference in inner freedom between the people wallowing in self-doubt and those who have become world-class.

World-class performers lived freely and they had coaches who helped them develop the skills, their own skills, to do so. Other people seemed to give away their inborn freedom to others, to coaches and parents and teachers who knew only a few ways to live. They learned fear from these people and in doing so, gave away their freedom. They tried doing what they were supposed to do in the belief they would be rewarded with freedom sometime down the road, freedom they were born with, but gave away.

When I was a junior in high school, my coach was very hard on me. As one of two returning players, he worried I would rest on my expectations, that somehow I had earned the right to start based on my previous year. So he stuck me on the third team in pre-season. He challenged me, threatened me, yelled at me, even mocked me. I responded with anger, anger I released in the way I played. For me this worked. I was relentless on defense. I dove after every ball. Worked my tail off in every practice.

The night of the first game, I walked in the locker room and saw my name in the starting line up. He just smiled at me.

By the time I was a senior, I had become good enough that he allowed me to run the team. He had prepared me to play as best I could, with the knowledge he had to share. He forced me to seek out the best players in the area and even some other coaches. I was again MVP and recruited by some of the top schools in the country, though I was not an All American or anything like that. One legendary NBA coach called me the best player in the area that year.

He taught me what I needed to play *free*, to be free doing the thing I loved most. His voice was not in my head and this freed me to respond to what was happening in front of me. This seems to me to be the purpose of coaching.

Sadly, though, I also had only learned one real response to being challenged — anger, which I did not express or impose on others. I simply held it in and when my college career did not pan out, I was left only with the anger. I knew nothing else.

Good coaching is about preparing someone and then setting them free with the skill to do work and to grow at the same time. I heard this over and over in my interviews. I hear the opposite in one-on-one work with people having a hard time. These people are following a script, tuned into a powerful story they cannot let go of because of the value they place on their coaches.

It's hard to apply this idea of freedom but it can be done. A coach's results matter as much as the person or people they are coaching. As someone in charge of the training of heart surgeons, part of my job is overseeing the education process with one goal in mind, a goal defined by the people who make the rules, who decide if a training program will be reaccredited. At the end of the training my boss must sign a document stating that our residents can act as independent heart surgeons. We must follow up to ensure this is the case after they leave training and document their success.

In other words, they must be able to not only do what we taught them as far as technique goes, but we have to prepare them to learn what is yet to be discovered, to learn new ways of doing things. The greatest obstacle to this is the value they place on what they learned from their coaches.

In almost every interview I did of great performers, they told me about the one person in their life who taught them about freedom, whose goal was to help them rise above the coach and what he knew. One college coach actually told me that he wants his players to learn how to learn because if they settled for what he could teach, eventually they would be trapped and therefore not be free to continue doing what they do. Imagine if your heart surgeon could only do what he learned twenty years ago.

The people I do one-on-ones with are trapped by the stories of the people, afraid that by rejecting what they learned they are also rejecting the people who taught them.

An Olympic Gold Medalist described his coach best, echoing what I'd heard from other world-class performers:

> "He was a Marine; he was a sniper in Vietnam. First, he has a sense of team, from having to depend on everyone around him to get the job done. But, second, as a sniper he had to depend on his own skills and the things that he had learned, for pure survival. If he screwed up, he was dead. He had to make decisions while he was in Vietnam that were life-threatening decisions, and he had to make them on his own while he was in the jungle … some of that he passes on to his swimmers: the trait of self-dependency. I think he creates an environment, a team environment, that's based on each and every swimmer's self-dependency. Or vice versa, he expects everyone to be self-dependent within the team environment. They're equally important.
>
> One of the things he gives all his swimmers is the ability to trust themselves when it comes clutch time. The closer we get to a meet, the more freedom he gives us. He develops an atmosphere of trusting yourself and making your own decisions. By the time we get to the meet we're doing everything on our own."

I asked him how he knew what to do and he replied that it came from being free to try new things, to test them in practice, and to explore when he felt something needed to be done.

When it comes to coaching for feel or through feel, it seems to me that there is one goal. To allow people to feel and then to explore what they feel. What so many people perceive is dangerous about doing what we feel is the consequences and unpredictability of impulsiveness. Good coaches help eliminate impulsiveness, but not spontaneity. Not-so-good-coaches eliminate impulsiveness by not allowing the people they coach to feel.

Exploring what you feel means testing it, gathering data or evidence that shows you that what you feel informs your energy to do work — or not. This means the freedom to do so. In sports this is often done in the off-season. In business it might mean doing it on your own time. Effective leaders and coaches in business, however, build this into the everyday lives of their employees. The freedom to wonder, feel, and explore. Research and development. My experience is if I tell someone what they feel is stupid or wrong, it increases what they feel and it becomes negative energy, energy wasted on work not done.

If, however, you allow someone to try something and it works, they appreciate what they've learned. The leader or coach learns too. If what they try fails, you gain credibility with them. If the result is somewhere in between, you work with them to rethink what they felt, to shape into work. In doing so, you help them see the value of feel instead of filling their head with stories.

In each case, they will learn and remember the lesson of *feel* and this in turn develops their ability to use that skill.

One of my friends was Associate Director of Coaching Development for the United States Olympic Committee (USOC) for ten years. We talk often about what he learned from that experience and how he applies that to his life as a father of three children. He echoed all of these sentiments, that freedom is the key, that feel matters. He wants his kids to be able to be independent thinkers and feelers.

What about discipline and rules? You may be thinking, "Surely we cannot allow people to do only what they feel." Except we must, within certain rules or principles. People are only free to do so if they know the rules or principles of the organization or team. They should know the meaning behind them. It's a lot like spelling. Knowing the rules of spelling, even knowing the principles of Latin, allows us to know what we are free to do and use those rules to become more free, maybe even learn more languages.

I saw Jackson Browne perform one night and he said when he was a child his mother told him, "Discipline is freedom, freedom is discipline." What I think he meant is that by knowing the rules, knowing what it takes is in its own way freeing. Break the rules and there are consequences. If, however, the rules are arbitrary or make no sense, if they are simply an expression of someone's personality, they are oppressive.

Sport philosopher Eleanor Metheny said:

> *"During the past ten years, I have talked with many men and women, and many boys and girls, about their interest in sports. In those conversations, I have heard many explanations, but always, sooner or later, I have heard the word 'freedom.' Freedom to go all out, holding nothing back, freedom to focus all the energies of my own mortal being on the voluntary performance of one self-chosen human-action, freedom to experience myself at my own utmost as a whole-hearted fully motivated, fully integrated, and fully functioning human being."*

The most interesting thing about these words is that Metheny said the freedom came from the clear set of rules that sport provides. The freedom exists within the rules, because of the rules. And the rules of sport change to keep that freedom alive over time. They are adapted.

The root word of discipline is disciple. Being disciplined means being a disciple of something or someone. It has nothing to do with hard work. It has to do with knowing and following something to the best of your ability.

Work requires being a disciple of work, of finding meaning and using that meaning to move and grow in life. My own belief based on my work is that *feel* is an important part of finding and knowing meaning and therefore of work.

Coaching is about helping others live *free* by developing the skills to do so.

In talking about applications and coaching, I cannot give you techniques, but I can offer some questions to consider.

1. What are the rules or principles your charges need to know? How do you help them know them well enough to find the freedom they provide? How do you point out when they break them?
2. How much control are you willing to give up? What and how much are you willing to risk?
3. How do you define meaningful movement or work? How do you communicate this to your charges?
4. How do they define meaningful movement or work? How do you know this or learn this from them especially if they're not sure?
5. How do you explore their ability to feel, instruct their skill to feel? Is there time or experiences built into the way you operate to allow this to happen? How do you respond when someone feels something he or she needs to explore?
6. Most importantly, how do you benefit from their success? From their freedom, freedom that comes from highly developed skills to do the work they value?

In the end, great coaching is never about the coach alone. Curt Tribble and I never focus on teaching because that is too narrow a definition of what we do. We help people learn, and the best learners often do it on their own. A good coach facilitates and inspires learning.

As Winston Churchill said, "I do not always enjoy being taught, but I love to learn."

My own philosophy on coaching is when individuals come to me for help, the goal I have in mind is to increase their freedom. I want to increase their skill to recognize what is in front of them as well their ability to respond to it. This includes increasing their range of choices.

If you coach people in a technique, if they can learn only from you, you might add one or two ways of responding to their arsenal. But if you teach them to learn, they can grow without you. They are free to find what works, what enables them to do work, long after they've left you.

Coaching can increase a person's knowledge to do something. Good coaching can increase wisdom that allows someone to choose and use knowledge in the best way possible for the situation. Coaching can provide information. Good coaching informs energy, summons forth positive energy, to do the work of our lives.

The main focus of this book is *feel* because, in my experience, feel is too often left out of what we teach, what we coach for. Coaching for feel increases wisdom because it increases the freedom we have to choose, to make decisions.

In medical training, it is often said that the most difficult time of a physician's life are the first five years after they leave their training program. Why? Because physicians feel responsible in a way they have never experienced before. I've spent a lot of time with surgeons after they've left training deal with the feel of being completely responsible for patients in a way they never have before. This is all about feel, dealing with failures that can result in someone dying.

Coaching for feel, with feel, means setting someone free to fail in a way that allows them to deal with the feel of failure. Coaching for feel means helping someone rise above their feelings of judgment so they can feel what is truly in front of them. If a surgeon loses a patient in the morning and then has to operate again in the afternoon, he or she must be able to learn from the failure and walk back in the operating room that afternoon, free to do the best work for that patient.

In a groundbreaking book, author Charles Bosch, spent three months following a surgical residency. Bosch found the difference between the mediocre, middle of the road residents and surgeons never admitted mistakes, believed they did no make many mistakes. In contrast, the residents and surgeons who people agreed were the best said they often made mistakes, had doubts. They felt this all the time, but saw it as healthy, keeping them accountable for their performances.

My experience tells me that these people had an expanded perspective, something they probably learned from someone they respected, someone who knew that they would fail and feel no matter how good they were.

In the end, this can only be achieved by teaching freedom because the flip side of freedom is responsibility. Good coaching facilitates wisdom by helping others experience and know that freedom and responsibility are siblings.

DOUG NEWBURG

I CANNOT TELL YOU HOW MANY DISCUSSIONS I HAVE HAD WITH PEOPLE IN UPPER MANAGEMENT WHO SAY THAT HOW SOMEONE FEEL IS NOT THE COMPANY'S RESPONSIBILITY AND NO ONE EVER ARGUES WITH THEM. THE REASON BEING I THINK IS BECAUSE PEOPLE MIGHT AGREE THAT THEY DO NOT HAVE A RESPONSIBILITY TO THE EMPLOYEES TO CARE ABOUT HOW THEY FEEL (THAT IS MORE AN ETHICAL QUESTION), BUT IF A "FEEL" GIVES A COMPANY A COMPETITIVE ADVANTAGE OR DISADVANTAGE, THE RESPONSIBILITY IS TO THE SHAREHOLDERS TO CREATE THE PROPER FEEL. I DO NOT BELIEVE PEOPLE TALK ABOUT THIS ENOUGH EXCEPT IN BOOKS AND RARELY DO THEY SAY IT AS A RESPONSIBILITY TO SHAREHOLDERS.

Responsibility

RESPONSIBILITY

*F*reedom and Responsibility are siblings. There's a fine line it seems to me between responsibility and obligation. We noted earlier in Chapter 9 that obligation becomes an obstacle to experiencing resonance or the kind of feel that individuals have within them that allows them to perform at their best.

In management seminars with business people, if we now move the discussion from coaching to business management (acknowledging that there are many overlaps), I often hear people say, "Well, this is all fine and good, but I have *responsibilities*! If it weren't for my family, maybe I could do what I really want to do or feel the way I really want to feel, but I have to pay the mortgage and put the kids through school and provide for my wife (spouse)."

My first reaction is cringing. I'll say, "Wow, I'm glad your wife and children aren't here to hear you say that. Because what you're saying is that they are millstones around your neck and are holding you back. How does one live that way day-to-day and not begin to resent?"

It causes me to think about my own spouse, Susan. When I married her, she couldn't ask the next person in line what time of day it was. She had been hammered her entire life into believing that everything was "her fault." When the dog bit her, it was her fault for being too close to the dog. If there was ever a dispute with a teacher, it was her fault and the teacher

was right. At home, at church, and at school, "they" were right, and she was always wrong. At 24, when we met as "adults," she clearly lacked virtually all of the freedoms that Doug described in the previous chapter.

Over the last 30 years, we have learned enormously from each other. Gradually it dawned on me as I studied human behavior in organizations at Harvard and came home to Susan in the evenings, that if she was to become her own person, she would have to learn to be free, free to express her feelings, free to do what she wanted to do, free to experience life as she wanted to experience it.

The discipline that she'd been brought up with had destroyed her freedoms. Let it be known that she had ADHD as a child (and as an adult — it doesn't go away), and this made those around her strive all the more to "control" her with discipline.

This reminds me of a new filly my dad bought one time when we were living in Idaho. She was a beautiful thing, a kind of reddish brown color with white stockings and a white face, and a frisky spirit. She'd run wildly around our three acre pasture (the fence of which I had to paint white regularly — my LEAST favorite chore of all growing up). In fact, although none of us had the words to describe this at the time, she seemed to be a little ADHD. Skittish. A flying leaf would send her running around the pasture. Hard to train. Wouldn't come to you. Wouldn't take the halter or bit. Wouldn't allow a blanket on her back.

So my dad sub-contracted out the training — or as some horsemen will say, "breaking" of the filly. I remember how difficult it was to get her into the trailer. That took an hour or more before she finally hopped, kicking, into the trailer. Then, the tail lights disappeared down our cottonwood-lined lane.

I was eager to see how she'd come back. I imagined she'd be all twinkly of eye, energetic, but more — what — poised. Refined. Elegant instead of wild. Like the disciplined line in the love story, *The Dot and the Line*, that my girlfriend at the time had given me.[1] Wild squiggles don't attract the girl, rather the disciplined freedom of expression that comes with knowing geometry was much more dazzling than unruly spaghetti.

Four weeks later the big day came at last. We were all there to greet our filly who'd been sent off to "charm school." When they lowered the ramp and backed her out, I didn't recognize her. She was dead on her feet. There was no light in her eyes. She stood motionless, head hanging down. The body was there, but the filly was not. I could see scars around her face, which now looked well-aged beyond her years. She had been beaten into submission. There was no energy in her.

In fact, she was ruined. You could ride her, but she wouldn't move, she'd just stand there. It was sad, depressing, and boring and soon thereafter dad sold her.

I never knew who that trainer was. I'm glad I never met him. I only knew him by the work he did, by the way the horse that left us and came back to us changed had been destroyed in the flesh.

I think Doug was lucky to have enough spirit inside of him that his coach didn't destroy him as a high school player. I wonder if he could have survived, emotionally and spiritually, if he'd played for that man another five years.

I know that my young bride, Susan, was a mirror-image of that filly when we got married.

Unfortunately, I see a lot of people like that in business. During the course of a seminar, they may be able to generate some enthusiasm, and yet you can tell there's a deep-seated underlying cynicism or skepticism

---

[1] N. Juster, *The Dot and the Line: a romance in lower mathematics*, Chronicle, 2000.

that pervades the room. Yeah but, they say, we're not allowed to behave that way. Again, the reason is, as I have tried to explain earlier, is that their managers are operating out of a Level Three assumption that "professionals will do what they have to do regardless of how they feel."

Somewhere in our third or fourth year of marriage, I began to realize, slowly Susan will say, that you cannot control others completely. If you try, you kill their energy; you destroy their freedom; and then you're left wondering how to motivate them.

I began to relax my death-grip on many Level Three assumptions that I'd been raised with. "Work before play." "A wife should submit to the wishes of her husband." "Children should be seen and not heard." "Children should obey." "A good worker does what he's told." "Always do more than you're asked, not less." "Do it right the first time." "Clean your plate." "Families should vacation together." "Wives should stay home and take care of the house and children."

How does one begin to question unexamined and even deeply held assumptions of which one is *unaware?* It's never easy, I suppose. In my case, Susan was an enormous help. She'd say things like, "You cannot argue with my feelings. They just *are*." "You don't see me." "We have to talk *now!*" Finally one day, "I'm leaving." *That* got my attention. My parents were divorced and I didn't want to go down the same path.

One day she said she wanted to go on an Outward Bound. That was a three-week trip into the wilderness with a backpack carrying everything you need to survive. Off she went. I wondered if she'd come back more like the filly or more free. I didn't understand why she wanted to do it.

When she got back, her eyes were *on fire!* She literally smelled like the woods, her skin was brown and smelled like bark — and that was *after* her one shower on the way home. She reported that for the first two weeks, she was praying that I'd "feel her vibes" and come rescue her in a helicopter. Then, on the next to the last day of the trip, she had to climb a 250 foot cliff.

250 feet means three 80 foot rope pitches. So you have to climb in a harness hooked into this belay line, then transfer to another one, and so forth. All the way up, she was yelling, "I can't do this!" But she kept moving.

Near the top, she said, there was an outcropping of rock that overhung the cliff face by five or more feet. She had to go over backwards and climb out and then up. She tired. Her fingers cramped. Her body was trembling. Her belayer told her to let go and hang for a while to rest. She was afraid, but she did. Then, to her surprise, she re-engaged, grabbed onto the rock and climbed out and up and over onto the top of the cliff.

She shouted out a word she'd never said before in her life. I wasn't there, but as I listened to her tell the story, I could see and feel the energy in her and I could imagine the scene. Like Rocky standing on the top steps in Philadelphia. Like Daniel Day-Lewis running up the rocky trails in *Last of the Mohicans*. In fact, her Outward Bound was held in the same spot as that movie was filmed.

Susan went on to another Outward Bound and then to crewing on a British tall ship, climbing 100 feet into the yardarms, among other things, to reef the royal top sails at night in a 30-mph rainy gale. And she has blossomed into a very self-aware, confident, capable, vivacious, gorgeous adult human being. That I may have had something to do with that is my proudest accomplishment in life even though it doesn't appear on my resume in any way.

All of which is to say, when managers persist in perpetuating an un-examined belief they have about how people are supposed to behave and act at work, far too often they are, perhaps unintentionally but none-the-less inexorably, sucking energy out of their people.

So how does one answer the 20- or 30-year management veteran who says, "I can't do that resonance thing. I have responsibilities!"

I think the answer is that you may end up doing the same thing you're doing, like when Curt went back into surgery the afternoon after a patient died, but you can do it with a very different mindset, and that difference makes ALL the difference. Do you come at your work from an obligatory mindset or a choiceful mindset? (See Figure 33.1.) The obligatory mindset says to itself, "I have to do this." The choiceful mindset says to itself, "I get to do this."

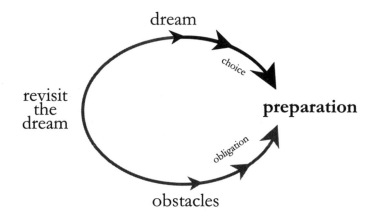

Figure 33.1. Dealing with responsibilities

If you can learn to revisit your internal life's dream, that is, how you want to feel, and make your choices about work from that perspective, the data Doug's collected would suggest that you can do at least three things at once: you can ramp up your own energy level, you can ramp up your performance, and you can feel more free about the whole thing.

I've been working on this for 12 years now since Doug asked me, and 700 others that night — how do you want to feel? It's made a huge difference in my life, in my relationships, and in my professional productivity. Doug's interview data and my experience say, "It works."

So, my answer to those of you who would say "You know, if it weren't for my family and other responsibilities, I could do this" is "You'd better figure out how to live your life in your resonance, whatever that is, because if you don't, there's a real danger you'll be undermining not only your experience but also be teaching your spouse and children that what they should do is to suppress their feel and do what they're supposed to do. If you don't figure that out before you die, you'll be missing out on what could have been an ocean of high-energy experiences and the opportunity to *show* your family and your employees what life and work *could* be like. But, hey, it's *your* life. You choose."

EPICTETUS

 GOD HAS ENTRUSTED ME WITH MYSELF.

Respond-ability

Respond-ability

I first met Jeff Rouse in the winter following the 1992 Summer Olympics. I was interviewing him as part of my dissertation on world-class performers. I didn't know at the time we would become good friends and that I would play a part in preparing him for the next Olympic games.

As the world record holder in the 100 meter backstroke, he had expected to win Gold in 1992, then retire. Things didn't work out that way. He took the Silver Medal, and in his eyes he let down his country and people he cared about.

As I grew to know him, one thing about Jeff became clear. He cared deeply about doing the right thing and about what other people thought. He had high expectations of himself and many of them were around coming through for others. So when he lost his race in Barcelona, he felt awful, felt he'd let down a lot of people.

The day following his Silver Medal win he had a responsibility to fulfill, one he was not looking forward to. He led off the 4×100 medley relay, a race the U.S. had never lost in international competition. He was dead tired and scared. He did not want to race and even thought about pretending to be sick.

I've told this story to thousands of people. Then I ask them, "What would you tell Jeff to help him succeed?"

Quite often the answer I hear is to remind him of his duty, of his responsibility to his country, to those who supported him. Some people tell him to suck it up.

This raises the question of what responsibility really is. Who exactly did Jeff have a responsibility to? And what was the best way to fulfill it?

After we met, Jeff and I talked about this frequently. He seemed to everyone like a very responsible guy. The more we talked, the more I realized how much pressure he felt from that responsibility. We talked about how real any of it really was.

In the end, it came down to one thing: *respond-ability*. How able was he to respond to the things he felt were truly important? He needed to take control of the expectations others had of him and those he had of himself. We spent time separating the athlete from the person. How he swam would not determine what kind of person he was to the people who were part of his life.

No matter what responsibilities Jeff felt as a swimmer, there was one thing he could do — swim the best he could. He surrounded himself with people who knew and accepted him a swimmer *and* a person. Those who saw him as only a swimmer would forget about him soon enough. Preparing for the 1996 Atlanta games, we spent time helping him get clear on what was a true responsibility and what were simply expectations imposed by others that he was accepting to no real gain.

In working one-on-one with world-class performers and those who seek to be world-class, this notion of responsibility and respond-ability is an ongoing focus. I learned this first from Jeff. Take control of your responsibilities and develop your ability to respond. Too often people take on responsibilities without knowing if they can actually respond properly. I know a fair number of people who define being responsible not by how well they fulfill their responsibilities, but how many responsibilities they have. I strongly encourage people to make sure they accept only those responsibilities to which they have the ability to respond.

We are each born free. We are given certain gifts, talents and abilities that when developed become our personal tools to sustain our freedom. Respond-ability is one of those gifts, offering us a way to respond to the needs of the world and people around us. In my interviews and in my personal experience, the people who do this best also help others sustain *their* freedom.

Respond-ability is all about developing your skills to sustain your freedom. If you choose not to, then you will be less skilled and less free.

I don't mean to imply we are always in control of the responsibilities we have. Sometimes we are delegated responsibilities we have a commitment to keep. Other times, we took on responsibilities before we realized we were taking them on for the wrong reason. Perhaps you adopted a dog before you learned you would be traveling frequently, or the mortgage is larger than the income you and your spouse can now afford. These are real issues and ones you know can't be ignored. I simply ask you to develop your skills, to discover your easy speed, to live freely, to feel free.

Jeff's teammates in Barcelona reminded him not of his responsibilities, but of his freedom, of his ability to respond to his loss. They reminded him of the skills he had to live freely even in the most difficult moments, the most public moments. They reminded him to swim the way he swam to get there in the first place. He needed to focus on what he could control, what he could feel good about, and ultimately who he was — a free man. With that perspective he swam with *easy speed*, broke his world record in the 4×100 relay, and won the Gold.

In Atlanta, Jeff was better prepared. He knew he was there to swim both as an individual and on the relays. He told the press he would talk to them *after* his races. He was prepared for things to go wrong like they had in Barcelona when the bus broke down or things were delayed. He was ready to respond. As a result, he won the Gold in the 100 meter backstroke ... *and* in the medley relay.

Several years later, after leading a workshop for a large organization, I received a call in my hotel room from Larisa, the company's vice president of marketing. She told me she was struggling with her job. I quickly realized she was having trouble doing her work, not her job. Much like with Jeff, I needed to make that distinction clear.

She had grown up with a military father whose voice continued to play in her head. She was very good at what she did. She loved the creativity that marketing allowed her. When she could find a place within herself where her creativity could become wonderful marketing it felt like the *easy speed* Jeff described. She created, she thrived, she did work. So why couldn't she get there?

Like Jeff, she was trying to live someone else's definition of responsibility and as a result, she was unable to respond to the obstacles she faced. A rebel as kid, she caught herself embracing her Dad's version of responsibility when she dealt with her children. Something I'd said in the workshop hit her hard. She feared she was becoming her dad and it scared her.

We talked again for months in the same way Jeff and I did. She made observations, collected her own data. My job was to get her to play her game, to do her work, not the work of others. I kept repeating, "NEVER allow your job to become more important than your work." She had simply lost sight of her work.

She re-found her work by collecting her data. Her children not only brought out a side of her like her dad, they also helped her stop listening to voice in her head, a similar voice to the one telling Jeff he needed to win. She told me about watching her son paint, something he did often in his room alone. She realized this was his response, how he found his own easy speed, how he wanted to feel — and it provided her a metaphor for she could also respond. In the past, she'd considered his painting a waste of his time and in those moments her dad's voice came out of her mouth. "Do your homework." "Clean your room." "Get ready for practice. Yes, you have to go." That night, she understood her son's canvas was the canvas where he was discovering his own gifts and developing them into skills that nurtured and sustained his freedom. He was doing this so he could respond to the world in his own way, something she'd never learned. She realized that she had this at her job, this canvas if she would just revisit it when she needed it most.

Jeff and Larisa had been trying to be responsible in ways that interfered with their ability to feel free. I informed their energy in a positive way by getting to know them and helping them get to know themselves. You cannot sustain your freedom by oppressing someone else. You maintain your freedom by acting responsibly.

David Bruce Ingram, a University of Chicago philosophy professor said:

> "To the extent that you don't examine your life, you don't own it. It's not yours, but someone else's. It means that you do something because that's what everyone else does, because you've always done it that way, or because Joe Schmoe the big expert tells you to. But doing something for these reasons is not taking responsibility for your own life. You heard me right. Being morally responsible means you think deeply about the meaning of your values and the norms you hold dear. If you don't do that, you're not being adult. Being adult means that you freely- voluntarily and with forethought- take control over the values that otherwise stay hidden. So dig 'em up and examine 'em."

Jeff and Larisa fell into the trap many of us do. They mistook responsibility for the ability to respond. They confused energized information with informed energy. As the CIO of the Navy said: knowing our story, having our canvas and living from that space matters because when we are bombarded with a counter story, someone else's expectations of us, we have the skills to respond. Jeff and Larisa had made their jobs too important, jobs defined by others and they *felt* it above all. What they felt was not their responsibility. What they felt was their freedom slipping away. They needed to get better at responding well in the direction of their work, responding to their dream.

In Jeff's case, he won Gold. In Larisa's case she became a better parent, a great presenter and teacher and one of the most sought after marketing consultants in her national organization. She felt free for the first time in her life.

SIMONE WEIL

HUMAN BEINGS ARE SO MADE THAT THE ONES WHO DO THE CRUSHING FEEL NOTHING; IT IS THE PERSON CRUSHED WHO FEELS WHAT IS HAPPENING. UNLESS ONE HAS PLACED ONESELF ON THE OTHER SIDE OF THE OPPRESSED, TO FEEL WITH THEM, ONE CANNOT UNDERSTAND.

Power

POWER

*P*ower is the ability to get others to do what you want them to do. As such, power is often viewed as a "Level One" concept in that it is usually directed at what others do regardless of how they think or feel. To have power is to be able to get others to DO what YOU want them to do.

In the management literature, there are many classical sources of power. One can have power because of one's legitimate or legal authority. In this domain, followers do what they are bid because the king, the father, the policeman, the magistrate, or the CEO have the recognized authority to tell them what to do. People may not agree with or LIKE what they're being asked to do, but because the "leader" has this legal authority the followers respond. Typically in influence systems (simply, a system with an influencer and a responder and a mechanism between them) based on legitimate power, there is an implied threat. If you don't do as you are bid, I have the power to punish you in some way: throw you in jail, send you to your room, arrest you, or fire you. The superficial (Level One) nature of this influence system means that it tends to get lower levels of buy-in from others.

Buy-in is not a binary process. We can easily think of follower response as a continuum ranging from active resistance to passive resistance to apathy to compliance (while looking for loopholes) to agreement (I will do what

you ask) to engagement (I want to do what you ask) to passion (what you ask is my #1 thing in life). Legitimate authority tends to have a high proportion of responses on the lower end of this scale. This is why over history, people have revolted.

A second source of power is force or coercion. The "leader" may not have any legitimate authority, but because he/she is bigger, stronger, more powerful (holding the biggest gun), others will obey. Unlike the case in legitimate influence systems, force or coercion holds an *explicit* threat: you do what I ask or I will hurt you. Again, this attempt to influence is a superficial one, targeting only visible behavior and basically ignoring thoughts and feelings. And force with its kin, intimidation, tends to get low levels of buy-in and breed high levels of resistance and resentment.

The Buy-In Continuum

7. Passion ("What you ask is my #1 thing in life")
6. Engagement ("I want to do what you ask")
5. Agreement ("I will do what you ask")
4. Compliance (obey but look for loopholes)
3. Apathy (don't care one way or the other
2. Passive Resistance (going slow)
1. Active Resistance (revolution)

People can exert power over others if they have something that others want. This may be gold, money, title, position, benefits, even access to certain groups. In reward oriented influence systems, the central mechanism is an exchange — you give me something and I give you something. Usually it's money for time and talent. Reward systems only work when both parties have something the other wants. One problem with reward-oriented influence systems is that they tend to have superficial influence over others. Large numbers of people go to work to get a paycheck but don't really enjoy or invest in the work they're doing.

Bases of Power
1. Legal/Legitimate
2. Coercion/Force
3. Reward
4. Expertise
5. Referent

There is also a power based on one's expertise. That is, if another has an expertise *in something you want to be able to do* that person will likely have some power or influence over you. I love to play golf, so if Tiger Woods stuck his head in the door one day and said, "Hey, would you like to go to the range and hit some balls," I'd rearrange my schedule and go. I might have passive respect for people who are experts in a field that I'm not particularly interested in. I can admire their skills knowing that they perform well, but unless it's an area of interest for me, this respect probably won't change my behavior that much and so the irrelevant expert's power or influence over me would be limited.

French and Raven[1] also speak of referent power, or personal-based power, in which because someone has attributes that you want, you will emulate or try to be like him or her. This power is part of what creates cults, or fraternities, or secret organizations, or clubs. People want to join so they watch those who are "in" and try to be like them — and in so doing allow the "members" to have power over them. At the mid ranges of buy-in, this can lead to growth and development. At the higher end, it can lead to zealotry and blind loyalty. Sometimes referent power comes out in values-based organizations where the members agree to do what the organization asks so that they can join and be members in good standing.

---

[1] John R. P. French Jr. and Bertram H. Raven, "The Bases of Social Power," in *Studies in Social Power*, D. Cartwright (ed.), (Ann Arbor: University of Michigan, Institute for Social Research, 1959), pp. 150–167.

The desire of the individuals to *be* members is what binds them to obey the organization's rules.

In our attempts to influence others, we usually use a mix of these common power bases. We develop habitual patterns in those attempts so that we can characterize a person as typically using more of one power base than another. For example, a non-profit organization like a church might use referent power to get people to join, which then gives the church leaders legitimate authority over the new members. The leaders might then employ rewards (pay or promises of a better next life) or even coercion (obey or we'll kick you out) to keep the new members in line. If the new members come to be deeply convinced of the values of the organization, the need to apply rewards and threats disappears and it's the expertise of the leaders, their understanding and knowledge of the afterlife and how to get there, that binds the acolytes to the organization. This pattern is not a new thing; it goes way back in human history.

I'm not convinced, however, that every time someone obeys what another asks that leadership is at play. In fact, I assert that unless the follower obeys willingly and with full disclosure you cannot call this influence leadership. If the follower has to obey for personal safety or if the follower doesn't know what the leader's doing to manipulate the followers' decisions, it may be the use of power, but it's not leadership. Were Genghis Khan and Stalin leaders? To those who followed them willingly and without intimidation or deceit, yes. To those who followed because of fear or ignorance, they were dictators. We might call them generically "authoritors," that is, people in positions of authority. Whether or not an authoritor is a leader or not depends, in my mind, on the reasons why the followers respond.

Here again, feel is the critical watershed. If as a follower you feel manipulated, threatened, coerced or forced to do what the "leader" wants you to do, it's not leadership. It may be the use or the abuse of power, but it's not leadership. If you choose to follow because you like where the leader wants to go without fear of retribution, then the "leader" has convinced you fair and square and you could call that leadership. All power is not leadership but all leadership is powerful.

Suppose that you're on a team. You "have" to go to practice. The coach yells at you and tells you what to do. You realize that left to your own devices, you probably wouldn't work out as hard as you do as when the coach is yelling at you. Maybe. My guess is that unless a) you love the activity/sport, b) you respect the coach, and c) you want to get better at the activity/sport, you won't have the stamina to continue going to practice. People tend not to persist in doing that which does not feel good to them (see Figure 35.1).

Often those in positions of power grow impatient with the process of connecting with people at a deeper level, so they resort to intimidation, force, coercion or incentives/bribes. While they may get the short-term results, typically it's not world-class and it's not sustainable. Power without attention to feel is doomed to fail. It's just a matter of time.

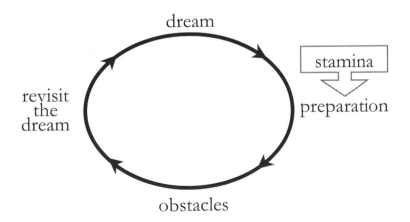

Figure 35.1. Finding the stamina to prepare to become world class

ALEXANDER GRAHAM BELL

WHAT THIS POWER IS, I CANNOT SAY. ALL I KNOW IS THAT IT EXISTS ... AND IT BECOMES AVAILABLE ONLY WHEN YOU ARE IN THAT STATE OF MIND IN WHICH YOU KNOW EXACTLY WHAT YOU WANT ... AND ARE FULLY DETERMINED NOT TO QUIT UNTIL YOU GET IT.

Powerful

POWERFUL

*A*lthough theorists have defined power for hundreds of years as, "The ability to get others to do what you want them to do," I believe power is the ability to do work well. And how you define *well* is, well, up to you.

What makes someone powerful? The ability to define and do their own work.

What makes someone powerless? The inability to define and do their own work.

World-class performers and organizations take energy, the raw human force inside each of us and refine it into work done well, into power. World-class performers seek out the people and environments that help them turn energy into power.

Positive energy moves something; negative energy is expended but results in no work being done.

The skill and ability to feel not only energized the people I interviewed, it took energy that had always existed in them and they turned it into power — at first to do the work themselves, to do what they felt, then to help them discover, grow, sustain their own definition of work. As they became better at music, business, caring for others, their power was increased because they helped others turn energy into power.

I am not making a moral argument about power. I am making a case for doing work… and as Adam Smith suggested, the best tool for us to know and do our work is ourselves. This idea that power is getting other people to do what we want implies that our work is somehow more meaningful, more important than theirs. Doing someone else's work for them in a way that diminishes our own work is not freedom. It is not capitalism nor democracy. It should not be tolerated.

Capitalism and Democracy depend on each of us knowing our own work, developing the skills to do that work, and the ability to act freely. Theoretically, both would function best if we all knew our work and knew how to carry it out so that each of us fulfills our own promise. We don't live in a theory, though. The world-class performers I interviewed found their own power by knowing what their work was as best they could. They knew that work because they discovered their own gifts that they developed into skills. Most of them had a place, a safe space, where they were allowed to make mistakes, to hone their skills, to touch the world so they could feel it. Ultimately that *feel* crafted back into touch, the ultimate power to do work.

The surgeon, who as a medical student, first touched a cadaver to feel the human anatomy so that when he cut into live, bleeding tissue, he had the touch, the power to heal, to do his work. The swimmer who touched the cold water for the first time with his toe, then dove in and felt the water embrace him so years later he could dance with it, the power of touch to create easy speed. The musician who gently touched the piano keys to feel the sound that with a touch developed over years, he turned into music. The CEO who went to business school looking for something, anything to light him up, touched by the way cereal boxes were placed in an aisle at the eye-level of a child, turning that feel into "a golden touch" that led to some of the most successful advertising campaigns in history. The mother touching her child for the first time, feeling his breath and movement, nurtured into the touch the child comes to depend on when everything else seems out of reach. That is the *power* I came to understand from the world-class performers.

They do not approach power as something they own or possess. It is not something they can use over or on other people. Likewise, it is not something *someone else* holds over them. Power is something they create or tap into and share.

I have talked with dozens of surgeons, hundreds of medical students, and many many patients. The one thing all three bring to the table is energy. Surgeons facing tough cases create energy that can manifest as worry and sometimes fear. Medical students often idealistic, tap into energy as they answer a calling they've known since childhood. Patients afraid of surgery, are energized by the shared clinical feel of their surroundings and the confusing maze of buildings they need to navigate when they arrive.

Their energy comes together in one place in the hospital as the patient waits, the surgeons prepare, and the students learn. Strong energy. However, the skillful surgeon, the educated patient, and the curious student working together can turn that energy into power in the place their missions overlap.

This is very different from the image of surgeons in decades past. The surgeon was the only one with the power. Yet the student had no less energy. Neither did the patient. Whether or not their energy was turned into power was seemingly irrelevant to the process.

Now we know the consequences of ignoring the energy, of leaving this energy unrefined, of believing and acquiescing to the idea that someone has power over us, is simply unsustainable.

In the case of patients, the power of a doctor can be limited to within the hospital, but powerful doctors know their real power is in their ability to turn the energy of their patients into the power to heal themselves, to thrive, not merely survive. For me, nothing is more powerful than seeing a patient turn the energy of worry, fear, doubt into the power to heal themselves, to get back to the things and people they love, and to do the work of their lives.

I use patient example for a specific reason. They often consider themselves powerless in the process. They often show up with their energy working against the healing process. It eats them up, makes sleeping difficult, and keeps them from moving.

The surgeon might have the ability to repair the damage to their heart, but if that is all that occurs, the patient's energy is rarely used to assist in the healing. The patient remains scared and timid instead of using his or her energy to recover and thrive.

If this is true for heart patients, then it is also true for most employees, for most of us no matter our role. We might believe our doctors, our bosses, our politicians have power over us, but the true source of power is within each of us. Can we turn our own energy into power? Can we use our own energy to do work well?

While some of the world-class performers I interviewed viewed power in the traditional way, in my time with them they talked more about power in terms of using their own energy and information to do work. They spend less energy worrying about the power someone else might have over them. This specifically showed up in how they talked about failure.

Many of them explicitly said, "I am not afraid to fail. I hate losing, but I am not afraid of it." They felt they could deal with losing or failing. This liberated them, allowed them to use their energy to do work instead of allowing it to fester or turn into negative energy. They sought out feedback and evaluation from people they trusted. They understood that seeking or inviting judgment would simply energize them, but with no useful information — that energy trapped inside them with nowhere to go rendered them powerless.

Powerful people and organizations turn energy into power, into work well done.

EDWARD ABBEY, *AUTHOR OF THE MONKEY WRENCH GANG AND DESERT SOLITAIRE*

DO NOT BURN YOURSELF OUT. BE AS I AM — A RELUCTANT ENTHUSIAST ... A PART TIME CRUSADER, A HALF HEARTED FANATIC. SAVE THE OTHER HALF OF YOURSELVES AND YOUR LIVES FOR PLEASURE AND ADVENTURE. IT IS NOT ENOUGH TO FIGHT FOR THE LAND: IT IS EVEN MORE IMPORTANT TO ENJOY IT. WHILE YOU CAN. WHILE IT IS STILL THERE.

ABUSE

*L*ove is a positive and powerful emotion. Freud once said that the purpose of life was "arbeiten und lieben" — work and love. Combining the two, loving what you do for work can be wonderful and essential for world class performance. But while love is a many splendored thing, it can also be abused. We see this in its extreme forms in the news from time to time; people who imprison their "loved ones" or who abuse them against their will. In the end, I think, love, like leadership, must be based on a voluntary response. If the other does not love you voluntarily and without pressure or need, how can you call it love? Likewise, if others do not follow you out of choice, how can you call it leadership?

The *abuse of feel* also comes in many varieties. One could argue that the world's young people seek the feeling of flow or resonance or of being in the zone. Some of them search legitimately through sports, academics, and building things. Others seek a faster, shorter term "high" through alcohol, drugs, video games, or promiscuity. It seems that the pleasure that emanates in the human brain through the release of dopamine after winning the 100-yard dash is not all that different chemically from the release after sex or the injection of certain drugs.

The problem is that these other sources of "flow" are counterfeit, that is, they don't lead to or fulfill all of the criteria of flow, especially the sense of growth and learning that occurs with true flow experiences. After a night

of short-term sensory binging one often feels smaller and even in pain. If you buy a sensation on-line or in a packet or at the amusement park, you emerge not having enhanced your ability to *do* anything or to *become* anyone larger. These are false and ultimately self abusing counterfeits for a real flow/resonance experience.

Take the love of work for example. You have noticed no doubt a thread running through our discussion here that in order to excel, it's important to engage in work/preparation/practice that you enjoy and find flow/resonance in. If not, the odds are that you'll not have the stamina it takes to become really good at the thing. So the upside to choosing work you love is that you'll likely get very good at it, perhaps even world-class.

The downside is that you may invest so much in your love, in your work, that other aspects of life begin to deteriorate to the point that they may affect your health and relationships.

Diane Fassel and others have described this phenomenon well as "workaholism."

" Hmm," you may say. "Is there such a thing?"

Actually, it's well recognized around the world. The Japanese even have a word for it, "karoushi" or working yourself to death.

Yes, workaholism can be as deadly as alcoholism — once laughed at — now recognized as a potentially deadly disease.

I'm sensitive to this perhaps because my father was an alcoholic for many years. There are reasons for his drinking I suppose, but they don't make living with the disease any easier. His father and his grandfather were alcoholics and likely possessed the D2 allele associated with addictive behavior.

My father, then, was genetically disposed, hardwired if you will, to addictive behavior. He smoked and drank — and worked very hard.

"You either do the job or you don't," he'd say.

"No excuses."

"Do it right the first time."

"Go back and do it right."

"Get away. You can't do that! Let me do it."

I remember him slapping my hand as a young boy trying to help him tie down the water skiing boat on the trailer. Jaw set hard, gritting his teeth, slapping my hand and telling me to get away.

Later, much later, I came to realize that he was probably self-medicating his biological and psychological demons with alcohol and tobacco. And *work*. Prodigious work.

I first encountered Fassel's workaholism scale[1] sitting in a hospital waiting room where I was about to have a EKG to see if my chest pains were related to cardio-vascular disease. (See Figure 37.1.) My father had had a major heart attack and a quadruple bypass at age 60, so I was a high-risk factor carrier. I remember sitting there and reading the following scale and going to myself, "Check, check, check, check, check, ... dang ..."

How far down the list do you get before the similarities begin to fade? I realized while reading this scale that I had long-standing habits of suppressing how I felt, never even considering how I wanted to feel, and had already long since exhibited many of these traits: hurrying, multi-tasking, unable/uncomfortable saying "no," "dreaming" constantly of work

---

[1] Diane Fassel, *Working Ourselves to Death*, Harper, NY, 1990.

- rushing, busy-ness, over-caring, rescuing
- inability to say "no"
- constantly thinking of work
- compulsive list making
- exaggerated belief one's own abilities
- no days off
- hours exceed 40 consistently
- other addictions begin: food, alcohol, etc.
- social life diminishes or non-existent
- give up relationships and obligations
- attempts to change fail
- physically worn out, difficulty sleeping
- periods of comatose staring into space
- blackouts at work and on the road
- chronic headaches, backaches, ulcers, etc.
- stroke, serious illness, hospitalization
- emotional deadness
- moral and spiritual bankruptcy
- death

working ourselves to death, diane fassel, harper, 1990

Figure 37.1. The work addiction scale

related issues, making lists to keep things straight, believing that I could (as my mom taught me) do anything, working through vacation times, working on weekends, stashing my work nearby (like an illicit bottle) so I wouldn't be caught without immediate access, spending less and less time with friends and "wasted time." At least twice, I have found myself two steps from the bottom.

In many ways we live in an increasingly workaholic world. The advent of mass communication through technology has created a flat world in which you know your competition is never sleeping. One must work harder and smarter just to keep up. Margins are eroding, so one must put in the extra effort to reach the "top."

Then I met Doug. He asked, "How do you want to feel?" My world view turned upside down. *Feel?* It never occurred to me to even ask that question. It was irrelevant. But what if you abuse your ability to feel, to enjoy, to thrill, to immerse for the sake of doing and achieving? You'll likely go far. Maybe become a CEO somewhere. Maybe become rich and powerful. But will you enjoy it? If not, something's amiss. If you do, more power to you.

There has been some evidence to suggest that many people who spend their lives focused on their work die shortly after they retire. In this case, Freud might have said simply "Arbeiten" and left the "Lieben" out. If you live to work, perhaps you're okay with that. If you do, are you deeply enjoying it? Do you thrill at the work you do? If not, beware. You may have developed habits over the years that can not only lead to your downfall/death but can also poison the attitudes of those around you.

I remember sending some material to my colleagues in preparation for a meeting and coming to the meeting expecting the same from my colleagues. One of them had nothing. She noted that she "had a life" outside of work and wasn't willing to put in the extra hours that apparently I was in order to do this preparation.

It was a comment that conflicted me. It stung on the one hand, as I wrestled with the question to myself, "Is my life way out of balance?" On the other hand, working had had gotten me through Stanford, Harvard, and the tenure process at Virginia. Where do you draw the line between love and abuse? Too much love is probably abusive and perhaps even self-destructive. It might even destroy relationships and families.

Another time, on a Thursday, I was working on my thesis and had a tight deadline to make by that Saturday at 2 pm. My wife was talking to me, I was aware of that, but what she was saying was not quite registering. She said louder, "We need to talk." I said, "Okay, but I have this deadline, and I have to get this done, so can we make it at 2:30 pm on Saturday?" The next thing I saw was the diminishing green light on my computer monitor. She'd climbed behind the desk and unplugged the computer. Her face appeared above the monitor and she said, firmly, "Now!"

Fassel offers steps one can take to get out of or avoid the self abuse that is workaholism. Evidences of that are shown below. Doug would say, "Wait a minute, the first step is to realize that you need to pay attention to how you feel." Many, mindlessly, even intentionally, ignore this and in so doing develop deadly habits.

For me, the big thing, the most powerful thing, the life-changing thing is: to pay attention to how you feel. And then to sort out how you *want* to feel, and then to nurture that and protect it and grow it. If you don't, my experience is, you can slip into the workaholic world, which is a world in which *feel* is abused.

Sadly, many of our institutions teach young people to behave this way. We teach our MBA students, for example, to work 'til late at night and often on weekends. We don't have Saturday classes anymore, and many of the alumni complain about that.

Soft!

Weak!

Less rigor!

Not the real world!

But it's not just in academe, for sure. I have clients who will ask to start the day's discussions with breakfast meetings, classes at 8 am, then run continuous sessions throughout the day until 10 pm at night. They do that in the name of driving up efficiency, productivity and trying to get the most out of one's fee.

But how can any human being learn, learn deeply, after a sixteen-hour day most of which was spent sitting on one's duff?

I have another client, a rare one, the only one in fact, who says to me,

"Don't work them too hard — nor yourself. We want you and them to enjoy this educational experience. If you and they are enjoying it, they'll learn more and you'll want to come back."

This guy is RARE in my experience in the business world. He's a gem client. He knows that you cannot abuse the way people *feel* and expect them to perform at a high level in any endeavor, even learning.

BENJAMIN DISRAELI

AS A GENERAL RULE, THE MOST SUCCESSFUL
MAN IN LIFE IS THE MAN WHO HAS THE
BEST INFORMATION.

Abusive

ABUSIVE

*H*ow do you feel what you never touch?

One NBA coach I interviewed told me he checks in with how he feels every half hour. Athletes often have routines to reset how they're feeling in the middle of competition. Surgeons play songs in the operating room that help them feel the way they need to feel when it will matter most. In each case, the world-class performers are choosing how they want to feel and for the most part they get in that neighborhood more times than not.

I hear counselors and personal coaches often proclaim, "You might not be able to control what happens to you, but you can always choose how you respond." Maybe this is true, but I know for certain there is no chance you'll choose a response you are not familiar with, that you've never felt. How do you feel what you never touch?

The most profound tragedy of abuse and about workaholism is that it imprisons us. We get stuck chasing not the feel, but a feeling. We get trapped into avoiding how we do not want to feel, playing not to lose. This is the hallmark of addiction. The high, the buzz, gives way to needing a fix ... and the fix needs more and more simply to avoid the pain of withdrawal. We shut off, our choices limited to only what we know. Our ability to feel, the skill of feel, hijacked by the pursuit of avoiding the pain.

I was working with a pro tennis player for months by phone as she was coming back after serious ankle surgery. She was in her late twenties and she wanted to keep playing on the tour because she loved tennis. I asked her to be more specific. What did she feel when playing tennis?

She was known for being able to run down every ball her opponent hit. She loved the feel of her speed, of what author Pat Conroy in *Lords of Discipline* called, "a nakedness of spirit, an absolute purity, a divine madness when I was let loose to ramble between the lines." Her ankle injuries had robbed her of this speed, the nakedness of spirit. Tennis was no longer what it had been for her years earlier.

She quickly understood what I was trying to help her see, help her do, and she embraced it. We had wonderful discussions, but they did translate onto the court. Had I known better at the time, I would have traveled to see her play, to watch her hit.

One night we were talking she sounded different. She had lost in the first round of a pro tournament and she sounded like a hardened person. The love, the joy was no longer in her voice. But the disappointment seemed gone as well — that disappointment a kid shows you when she whispers and bows her head. It is a disappointment that tells me she knows she can do better.

I assume what I heard that night was resolve, resolve that this was who she was as a tennis player and that if she just kept plugging, she'd get better. I decided I needed to take her back to the beginning.

"Why are you playing tennis?" I asked.

In the past conversation she would have simply told me she loved it. Loved how it felt, loved the sport, loved the routine and the lifestyle. Not that night.

"I want to prove to everyone I can still play," she replied.

There was a silence that I let hang. I could tell she did not believe that came out. I had been waiting for it.

We decided together that night it was time for her to retire, which she did. She went on to business school and then on to one of the big consulting firms. Soon she was calling me with a new challenge, a new opportunity. Over the years we'd kept our conversation about feel going. Then she was leaving her firm, looking for a new job and she'd hired a career consultant to help her find the right job. She went to one interview and then returned to the consultant to talk about it. The consultant told her that if the thought of doing the job did not make her sick to her stomach, she really should take the job. It was well-paying and with a well-known company. I almost fell out of my chair. She wanted to know what I thought. I didn't say anything. She understood. I told her she should get her money back from the consultant.

Several months later, she called me again to tell me about her dream job, the job she was preparing for which had come available sooner than she expected and she was the leading candidate. It was with an association that combined tennis with education for inner city kids. It was at the place she'd fallen in love with tennis.

Over the years we had many conversations about work, about what is expected of each of us, about what we expect of ourselves. More than anyone else I worked with, I saw the struggle in her to want to feel the way she wanted to feel. She understood how that was the best way to perform at a high level, but she also kept hearing the siren call of the storyteller, of the expectations of others, maybe of herself. It was hard to ignore despite her own experience with feel and the success it provided for her.

I can't say I understand workaholism. I cannot say I know what is abusive, but in my work, I know no matter how much I teach people about feel, we live in a world designed to keep us chasing something outside of ourselves. We live in a world in which power too often means getting others to do what we want.

I often find myself dumbfounded by people's willingness to abandon what they feel, their own personal data, to return to the call of the storyteller, to lives of, "doing what they're supposed to do." I will help people find their own feel, and then watch as they have successes they never imagined only to give it away to the storyteller.

My research, my consulting experience tells me that we were designed to feel, to develop our own ability to feel, so we specifically can transcend evolution's trick. I believe that with feel, we know what makes us happy which makes us less likely to be tricked. It is that knowledge, informed energy, which keeps us from abusing, from becoming addicted. As one CEO I worked with said, "Happiness is being able to feel the way I want to feel."

CANADIAN TRACK & FIELD
OLYMPIAN

YOU LOOK TO REPEAT THOSE MOMENTS
IN SPORT BECAUSE IT'S LIKE YOU TRAIN
FOREVER TO DO IT PROPERLY, AND WHEN
YOU DO IT PROPERLY AND YOU FEEL WHAT
IT FEELS LIKE TO DO IT PROPERLY, IT'S LIKE
"WOAH," YOU KNOW. THEN IT'S ALL WORTH
IT.

YOU'VE GOT NEXT

*A*t the gym when you lose or you're too tired to continue, you leave the court. The team(s) on the sidelines know they have "next." You stretch a little, hydrate, and take a leisurely hot shower. You feel good all over, even if you left everything on the floor. Then as you walk back out into the world, you stand taller, feel cleaner, stronger, and you glow from the inside out.

I just finished a two full-day seminar in Mexico City on teaching. It was a delight to spend 16 hours with 40 new colleagues, all of them very interested in improving their teaching craft. At the end of the two days, I was exhausted, but it was the good kind of exhaustion. It felt good. Especially since it was "pure," that is, pro-bono. We had two days of very good conversation for the sheer joy of it. I learned a lot. I believe they did, too.

I began the session as I usually do, asking them what their biggest challenges and issues were. These were university professors but their comments could have come, and have come, from practicing managers.

"How do you motivate people?"

"How can we interest our people in what we're doing?"

"How can I balance my life better?"

next

"How can I communicate better?"

"Should I/we change what we're doing? If so, how?"

Like managers all over the world, they agreed that how you feel affects your performance. They admitted to beginning their days with "What do I *have* to do today?" No one had ever asked them how they wanted to feel. We talked about their students. They surmised that they, too, began their days with "What do I have to do today?" They had never asked their students how they wanted to feel.

I see this all over the world — a huge irony between a universal understanding on the one hand that how you feel affects your performance and a universal acknowledgment on the other hand that no one has ever asked how you *want* to feel. It seems like a huge waste of human talent and energy — to tell people that the only thing that counts is results and that how you feel doesn't matter; you should just do what you have to do and suck it up.

How many people in the world are going to work daily with very low energy levels — trudging along in obligation? How many people in the world are going to work every day wondering what choices they can make that day and how they can *make* it a good day. People say, "Have a nice day." That's pleasant to hear. I wish they'd say, "*Make* it a good day."

Csikszentmihalyi's prison mates, some of them, did this in horrible conditions. The Mexican automobile assembly line worker he described did it despite mind-numbing work design.[1] Justin, the twenty-two year-old young buck "catcher-extraordinaire" in the best-selling short film, *FISH!*, understood that you *can* choose how you feel. The doorman at the Boston Marriott in Len Schlesinger's book, *The Real Heroes in Business ... and not*

---

[1] Csikszentmihalyi, Mihalyi, *Flow: The Psychology of Optimal Experience*, Harper & Row, New York, 1990.

a CEO among them, was often in the zone. These are not people in fancy jobs. These are everyday people.

Much of what we've talked about in this book describes how world-class performers, touring musicians, Olympic athletes, heart surgeons, high growth executives, and aircraft carrier landing crews have learned how to manage how they feel in order to improve their performance. And they note that the feel is its own reward. But you don't have to be a world record holder or a heart surgeon to ask yourself, "How do I want to feel today?"

You can figure that out. I hope you will be able to before you die. Then, if you can identify how you want to feel, then you can begin working on what it takes to get that. For me it's "light, unhurried and engaged." As I said, it took me 18 months to figure that out after I started trying. I've heard Doug's internal dream   but I'll let him tell you about that.

After you've figured out how you want to feel and how you can raise the probabilities of making that happen — you're likely to hit obstacles, not the least of which, in my experience, will be old habits. My hardware (genetics) and firmware (VABEs/memes) have been two of the biggest obstacles in my efforts to build my life more around feel. I have to keep reminding myself. Susan, the love of my life, also helps. I should listen to her more. She gets this better than I. But that's how you break through the obstacles — by continuing to come back to the internal dream, how you want to feel. It's an on-going process. But gradually I'm getting better at it.

I went today to see the Pyramid of the Sun northeast of Mexico City — a monument of the Teotihuacan people. My wife cautioned me against climbing it, something she'd done the year before. I had bi-lateral quadriceps tendon ruptures two years earlier while descending some stairs in Istanbul, Turkey. They had to drill holes in my kneecaps and tap in tiny pitons and then thread sutures through them and the shredded mop-end tendon masses to reconstruct my walking system.

I assessed the pyramid carefully. I tested several of the nearby staircases. On the Pyramid of the Sun there are 266 steps to the top, many of them uneven, with changing slope, and only partial hand rails/cables. I went to the top. My heart was pounding in the thin 7,000 foot air and from the high steps and exerting to lift my body. I rested periodically, and then continued on, one step at a time. Until … I was there.

It had rained that morning and the view was spectacular. Both stunning and sobering as one overlooked the Avenue of the Dead and realized the hundreds and hundreds of souls who were sacrificed annually on those grounds. The north-south/east-west "sacred" intersection lay below. The dry farms stretched out miles to the blue gray mountains surrounding. The neat frames of the related buildings and structures stretched in three directions — very unlike the Egyptian pyramids which are surrounded by sand, confusion, and were built as tombs of the dead. The Teotihuacan monuments were living structures with a thriving culture, much more like the Roman market that lay at the foot of the Acropolis.

There was a peaceful feeling standing atop the structure despite the people milling about and asking for pictures to be taken. I went to a quiet corner on the south side of the peak, to a narrow ledge there, and quietly performed my high form, the testing form for first dan black belt in traditional taekwondo, form 14, Chun Jang Hyung.

The regularity of the movements merged for me with the regularity of the ancient stone structures below me. The sun was bright but not intense. There was a gentle breeze blowing and I lost myself in the form.

I felt light, as if I could fly.

The faint sounds of the flute sellers below wafted up and made me feel like I was among the eagles. Despite our deadline to meet the tour bus, I was unhurried. I did not rush the form, but focused on the movements, only dipping for the one that requires one to kneel momentarily.

I don't remember seeing during the form. I do remember seeing before and after, but not during. As I felt the form come to a conclusion and realized that I was utterly engaged in it and its structure, I felt at peace.

It had taken me nine years to get to where I was allowed to learn that form. I had prepared fairly intensely. Indeed, there had been obstacles. Torn rotator cuff on the right side. Two ruptured quad tendons. Another torn rotator on the left side. Wife dropping out. But the feel — of being able to execute what I had prepared for 210 feet above a place that annually gathers 2,000,000 people in homage to feel — it was ... sublime.

Figure 39.1. Pyramid of the Sun, Teotihuacan, Mexico © Jim Clawson

When I finished, I was surprised to see what had been a very empty corner of the pyramid had accumulated 30 or more people. Two of them approached me and introduced themselves as students in an English class, and asked if they could fulfill an assignment by interviewing me. It felt a little odd to step back into "the world."

Later, I did another form — Number 11, Po'an Hyung, which is designed to be executed in narrow hallways — on another deserted corner of that top plateau. It was perfect for the narrow stone walkway that tumbled steeply down in front of me and rose to the rounded summit behind me. When I finished, I walked slowly to the staircase, trying to imagine how many hearts or heads or gallons of blood had washed down those stairways.

I descended slowly, thinking about the descent in Istanbul that left me lying on the sidewalk in excruciating pain and unable to move. On the flatter sections, I went straight down, but mostly, especially as the slope steepened, sideways, first to the left until that leg was tired and then to the right. Several sections have a cable to hold onto; many do not. I focused on each step and made sure each step, as in a form, was where it was supposed to be. Exiting onto the Avenue of the Dead, I turned right to meet up with our group at the base of the Pyramid of the Moon.

The plaza there is much more deserted. A few hawkers, some of our group, but mostly a large, open stone floored plaza with a 40- by 40-foot stone six-foot high platform in the middle. I climbed onto the platform and did one more form, number 12, Kebec Hyung.

There was an old man standing in the plaza, holding flutes for sale. As I finished my form, he began to play. He was about five feet four inches tall, and was wearing an old straw hat with frayed edges. The seams on his light blue shirt had also frayed so that the wispy threads floated in the light breeze. He had large bushy eyebrows, black, sprinkled with lots of gray. He carried a pouch over one shoulder, filled with simple, four-hole wooden flutes carved in various forms of birds.

But his music! My god, his music!

The tones were high, lilting, with varied cadence, like a bird soaring on the wind, like Doug's pelicans floating over the surf, like eagles wheeling above a desert.

I gave him less than what a DVD costs and asked him in my haltingly bad Spanish if he would just play for me. I don't need to buy a flute, just play for me. I sat on the top step of the platform, closed my eyes and he stood beside me and played.

The effect was electric.

One of my group came by and broke the spell to buy a flute. The old man had several types — one sounded like an eagle in the sky, one which he played most deftly sounded like the rushing of great waters or of air coming out of a Japanese mountain train tunnel when the train entered the other end.

He sang a song, too, standing beside me, unashamed, not embarrassed, acapella, for me, and ... and then we had to go. The tour guide, Roberto, was waving to us across the plaza. I stepped down onto the gravel floor and walked, feeling upright, after them.

After about 20 yards, I turned to the old man, and signaled again,

"Will you play for me?"

I walked to the corner of the plaza with my arm in the air, listening to his soulful tones dancing on the air. As I was about to turn to wave — he played the rushing waters flute, I turned and waved at him, now a hundred yards away, and he waved at me.

I felt at peace.

Light.

Unhurried.

Engaged, and

Connected.

Connected to him, to human kind, to our ancestors who built that place 1900 years ago.

***

I see millions around who don't understand the importance of feel. Who have forgotten how they felt as children or occasionally when it happens, are embarrassed. I see people all over the world in poverty and in wealth, in blue collar and in white collar, in this continent and in that continent, who don't understand this — how important it is to find your internal dream, to feed it, to protect it, and to let it work for you. This is sad for me.

Some of my students think I'm a fatalist. Quite the contrary. I find in Doug's research into the way in which life is powered by feel an enormously uplifting and optimistic message. Life does not *have* to be filled with drudgery. If you can figure out how you want to feel, and then protect that, and nurture it and use it, regardless of your station in life, you can feel a rising tide beneath you.

I'm all for discipline at Level One, doing what you need to do to feel the way you want to feel. As a lifelong academic, I'm indeed all for expansion at Level Two, conscious thought. Life's too short to learn all the things there are to learn. That said, I've become convinced, thanks to a former basketball player who embarrassed me on the pick-up court one day, that you *can* know your internal dream, that is, how you want to feel, and that if you can figure out what that is, if you can bring your resonance to everything you do, you can outperform your wildest dreams, whether they are world-class or not.

I'm done. You're next.

MALCOLM GLADWELL

HERE IS THE SOURCE OF THE PHYSICAL
GENIUS'S MOTIVATION. AFTER ALL, WHAT
IS THIS SENSATION — THIS FEELING OF
HAVING WHAT YOU DO FIT PERFECTLY INTO
THE DIMENSIONS OF YOUR IMAGINATION —
BUT THE PUREST FORM OF PLEASURE?
WHAT GRETZKY HAD WAS WHAT THE
PHYSICAL GENIUS MUST HAVE BEFORE ANY
OF THE OTHER LAYERS OF EXPERTISE FALL
INTO PLACE: HE HAD STUMBLED ONTO THE
ONE THING THAT, ON SOME PROFOUND
AESTHETIC LEVEL, MADE HIM HAPPY.

The Game with

The Game with No Name

*S*o you've got next, but next what?

As I began this chapter I struggled with what to write, not because I didn't know what to say, but because there seemed so much to say — and yet that betrays the most fundamental lesson I learned about world-class performance.

World-class performance, *greatness*, *excellence*, whatever words you choose, always contains one characteristic: *elegance*. Something as powerful as it is simple. And yet this is the hardest lesson of all to teach. It requires unlearning much of what we learned about hard work from people we trusted growing up.

I want to use this last chapter to share with you the elegance of the world-class performers I interviewed. You've got next, so let's start playing right here, *right now*.

The game begins with a simple, but difficult choice. What do you want to play?

I don't mean whether you want to play basketball or business or house or doctor or … I mean whether you want to play *outside-in* or *inside-out*. I finally understood this choice after years of consulting, of trying to share with other people what I'd learned from world-class performers in our interviews. This is the choice Jim confronted when he first heard me speak.

As I see it, there are at least two games from which to choose. They are both games we have experience with, games most of us have played in our lives.

They are the Game with No Name (inside-out) and The Storyteller Game (outside-in).

I call the first the Game with No Name because it is up to each of us to discover what informs our energy. For Jim it was, "light, unhurried, and engaged." For Jeff Rouse it was, "easy speed." For me it is, "elegance, as powerful as it is simple." I feel that when I am living out of my chest.

I call the other the Storyteller Game because it is the accumulation of stories from *others* playing in your head that informs your energy.

The secret I discovered is that world-class performers are not merely playing differently from the rest of us, not merely playing the Storyteller Game well enough to win it. They are playing a completely different game. They are playing the Game with No Name.

My biggest mistake early in my career was believing I could win the Storyteller Game, the "if I take the safe steady route and keep my nose to the grindstone, it will pay off down the road" game taught by those stuck in that life. I had heard early in life and then repeated, if you do what you're supposed to do, life will feel the way you want it to feel.

Even worse, I began to believe that the reward some people were trying to win was to *become the storyteller*, to have the power to make the rules, to live inside the heads of others, to be experts in the lives of others. People strived to make people respect them or admire them or even fear them. They believed they could actually earn the right to run the game for all of us.

Then something happened along the way. Two things actually. The first was I noticed that people who were truly engaged talked very little. When they did, they talked about how they felt, not about what they thought. Furthermore, feel was hard to describe, hard to talk about. They could feel it, but not necessarily share it. It took real effort to get at it.

The second thing was that I realized when people performed at their best, there was no voice, no storyteller playing in their head. There was silence and stillness and space. Another reason to call it the Game with No Name — when we play, there are few words, no names, just play.

In the Game with No Name, that silence, stillness, space presents itself as a canvas, a canvas where we create, as Yo Yo Ma said, "Something living."

Consider the following excerpt from *To Infinity and Beyond: The Story of Pixar Animation Studios* by Karen Paik.

> "Pixar's Chief Creative Officer, John Lasseter, suggested Pixar offices be furnished with simple wood-frame cubicles instead of elaborate and expensive office furniture, predicting animators would treat their space as an empty canvas anyway. The result? 'I'll admit I was skeptical coming into it,' said Edwin Catmull of Pixar. 'But the building turned out to be the most remarkable that I have ever worked in. You can feel the energy when you walk in through the front door.'"

It is this canvas, free of the storyteller, with space, stillness, silence waiting for feel to start building, painting, writing, doing work. It is the canvas for ideas that begin the process. Free to make mistakes, to learn, to decide, to erase, to begin again. It is this canvas that also demands data, requires accountability, not because of a need to judge, but to do work well.

World-class performers see the *can* in canvas. It is not a place of cannot. The canvas is not governed by rules imposed from the outside. The canvas is about discovering promise and honing the skills to fulfill it. It is not about having or owning. It is about making and creating. World-class performers make music, make champions, make great companies, and make the people around them better. World-class performance is about the creation of wellth — our personal health, wealth, and skills nurtured and grown, then woven into the universal power grid of human promise.

This is the total of my work, what I do with people. I help them access that space, their canvas. In my workshops, in my one-on-one consulting, I help people find a way to discover themselves and start playing. As one ninth grader told me after a semester-long program, "You created a safe place for us to discover and share ourselves at the same time others are doing the same."

In that space, on that canvas, we discover our gifts, our talents, our magic. We discover those gifts and talents, then we develop our skill in using them.

Feel, wonder, play, the ability to do work, our own work.

As we forge those gifts into well-honed skills, we grow. The more we grow the better we are at knowing what work is worth doing and how to inform our energy into the doing of work. The better we do this, the better ideas we create. The better the ideas, the better the dream that emerges.

The Game with No Name is finding that spot, that canvas and using it to develop our skills to identify and do work worth doing. We have the right, right now, to work and live from that place.

The challenge of the Game with No Name is the same as the other game.

The challenge resides in the storyteller who wants to tap into our feelings, to prevent us from using our ability to feel. The storyteller wants to fill that space, to disquiet the silence, and to rob us of our stillness. He wants us to be busy, to rush, to chase, to turn wonder into worry. The storyteller wants us to be consumers, not creators. The storyteller wants us to pursue, but never subdue. He wants us to feel empty instead of seeing our canvas.

In my interviews, one story kept coming up from the veterans, people who had regular jobs in their youth and who left those jobs to find success. They said in essence, "When I was looking for a job, companies were looking for people who wanted to settle down, who had families, who had mortgages. They knew they would not leave, that they were more stable for the company because they had obligations. Quite frankly, they viewed us as stuck."

That is the Storyteller Game, the not-so-golden handcuffs. Many of the people I interviewed left those jobs to create their own lives. I am not condemning owning a house or having a family. I just don't know anyone who wants to see those things only as obligations. The Storyteller's Game is about owning and having and consuming. Driven by fear, wonder replaced by the worries of having enough, of fitting in, of seeking approval. Endured, but never played.

Bobby Jones once said of Jack Nicklaus, "He plays a game with which I am not familiar." It is easy to wonder if world-class performers are also playing a game with which many people are unfamiliar.

Most of us know the Game with No Name personally because we played it as children. We played with focus. We played all day and it did not really matter what activity we played. We went to sleep dreaming about what we'd play the next day. Some of us even woke up early to go throw some more, shoot baskets some more, run some more, to get there before everyone else. We played with everything we had and limped home exhausted. Then we got up and did it again.

The true competition, as described by many of my interviewees, was between their vision and their skill to carry out that vision. It was the fit between their information and their energy. Did they have the best information they could have to make their energy do the work they wanted done?

These world-class performers found, as Malcolm Gladwell said, something that made them happy when they were doing it, not merely in the pursuit of something that would make them happy. Maybe they never lost sight of their spot, their magic, that canvas. Maybe they learned in childhood how to inform their energy into adulthood. Maybe they peeked behind the curtain and saw that the wizard was simply a man. Maybe they could see Santa Claus wasn't coming down the chimney, but that did not diminish the magic the idea made them feel.

If I've learned anything from the world's great performers it is this: live an aesthetic life, a life in which you think and feel simultaneously. *Making* requires thought and feel to work together. It requires the data and skill of *feel* and good thinking to use the data and skill wisely.

Every single performer I talked with spoke passionately about something they felt, something that resonated with them. It was something they could not own, something they could not buy. The rhythm, that *feel* they realized was something they made, something they created. In the creation, in the making, they saw the whole, found work worth doing. Musicians who started out making music, then building a studio, then producing. Athletes who saw the need to improve the engineering of their equipment working with manufacturers to create that harmony. CEOs who walked the aisles of grocery stores to understand their customers' experience. Doctors who made their patient's story part of the healing process.

They could not hold onto or possess the experience. They never even tried. They could make it, but never have it. And when they got in that place, when they beheld it, they were smart enough to enjoy it, to learn from it, to grow from it and to protect it and increase their ability to create it anew. They learned. They grew. They created. They made their world. That was the work of their lives.

Having is about spending. Making is about investing.

Having is static. Making is dynamic.

Having is about productivity. Making is about creating.

World-class performance is about risking what you think you have to see what you can make.

What I learned, what I want people to consider, is that the true energy crisis in our world might be inside each one of us. Without well-informed energy, we will struggle to know what work is worth doing and how to do it with power. Without that canvas, without the wonder of an Einstein, without the ability to feel, we are left playing the Storyteller Game as if we are stuck next to Bill Murray in the movie *Groundhog Day*, tricked into living the same day over and over believing that somehow it would turn out differently. We buy things we don't need and we consume things we cannot replace. Our energy feels like fear and worry and doubt and then eats us alive.

As Adam Smith said, the only property we have is ourselves and the results of the work we do. Why not use the best of ourselves to play, to know and do our best work? Why not develop our own gifts into the skills to do meaningful work? Why not give our energy only the best information?

And if *feel* does affect how you perform, how you work and play, why not feel your best? The best of the best have always been described as having a feel and the touch for what they do.

We've got next. *Let's play.*